Bedtime Stories
from
Shiloh:

Adventures

in

Faith & Trust

By Barbara Lovett

Table of Contents

Forward — 1

Dedication — 5

Chapter 1: How it all Began
Saved from Disaster — 9
Super Mom No More — 17
Raising Girls with Personalities — 21

Chapter 2: The Search for Shiloh
Norm's Vision — 31
Buying Property — 37
Finding Affordable Horses — 41

Chapter 3: God's Provision & Miracles
Diving and Losing Money — 47
Amigo — 53
The Concrete Miracle — 57
That's the Ticket — 61
The Player Piano & Washing Machine — 63
Up Close and Personal — 73
The Miracle of the Canada Geese — 79

Chapter 4: God's People
   God's Merciful Healing   87
   A Shower or Ministry?   95
   Beauty of the Butterfly   103

Chapter 5: The Angels that Got Hazardous Duty Pay
   Kicked by a Horse   113
   Fall from the Entryway   119
   Falling Off the Roof   121
   Log Rolling   123
   The Big One   125

Chapter 6: Lessons Learned
   God, Cars, and Me   137
   Secret to Quitting Smoking   147
   Sitting on God's Lap   149
   The Journey vs. the Destination   151
   The Big Fight   157
   God, Prayers and Sanguines   167

Chapter 7: The Legacy of Shiloh
   Our Darkest Days   173
   The Light Shines Again   183

Epilogue   187

Forward

If you were to ask me, "Why write a book about life at Shiloh?" I would have to tell you my wish is to express to the Lord and Savior my gratitude for how He has shown me His love and His faithfulness. I also want to encourage you, the reader, in your journey of faith and honor the wonderful God we serve. He isn't just a name in a book, or a far out unreachable God that we can't communicate with. We can feel His love and know His personality. He is real. He is caring, loving, and sometimes unpredictable (in a very exciting and good way). He is always there (even when I am not very attentive to Him). He is always looking out for my best, always lifting me up when I am down, and always letting me know that He has the right answers for all my questions about life. He is my best friend and never fails me. He is my awesome Father, showing me how fathers are supposed to be (I never experienced an earthly father). He is my Savior – the one I want to spend eternity with.

After reading these stories, you might ask, "Did God always answer your prayers?" Of course He didn't. At least, He didn't always do what I asked...and thank goodness! Many of my requests would have been disastrous for me. Many of them would not have helped me grow in faith or learn the lessons and principles I needed to learn. No, God is much wiser than that; He knew what I needed most, and that is what He always provided. As good parents, we don't always give our children everything they ask for–just what would be beneficial for them. As doctors say, "Do no harm". That is how God is.

In one of the following stories, I recall the time when I was sharing with a dear friend how I would be so glad when the lodge at Shiloh Ranch would be done, so we could really begin the ministry. This very wise friend said, "Wait a minute Barbara, you have this all wrong. Throughout all these years of struggling, you've built the ministry; it's a Spiritual process." After thinking about what he said, I realized that I would not have wanted God to just hand us a million dollars from the beginning and say, "Here, go build your ranch." That would have ruined everything. First of all, I wouldn't have been able to experience God's perfect plans, His faithfulness, or His exciting and wonderful personality. And with my personality, I would be so disappointed not to have these wonderful stories to tell.

Every time I had the opportunity to share some of these stories around the dinner table at the ranch, people would encourage me, "You need to write a book." And so I have.

    I probably never would have been able to do it if it hadn't been for some very good advice I received from a staff member. Each time she heard me telling these stories, she would say, "Let's write it down in a notebook—at least the name of that story, so you won't forget it." Years later I was able to use that notebook to start my writings. It was hard for me to get started but with the encouragement of my dear friend Ulla Lack, I began. But it was slow until my cousin, Jean Hollands motivated me. Actually, she "demanded" I set a schedule for writing and keep it. That was the push I needed. Thank you all so much.

Also, I could never have done it without my talented Editor, Kristina Detwiler. I am so thankful for her patience and encouragement. And to Norm, my melancholy husband who kept this sanquine writer from writing a "barely true story."

Dedication

This book draws upon the love, support, and encouragement of the Godly friends and guests of Shiloh Christian Guest Ranch who stood by us when we only had a vision (That must have looked like a mere dream in the early 70's) and stuck by us during the whole 25 years of ministering to hundreds and hundreds of families and individuals. It is dedicated to two of those saints, Bill and Barbara Westrate, whom God has raised up for this time and purpose of strengthening and restoring American families.

Bill first came to Shiloh in those early years when we only had the small cabin and barn. He and the rest of the youth group from Chicago were bunked in the hayloft of the barn. Before he left, he expressed a desire to help Shiloh develop further. Later he came back with his girlfriend, Barbara, to propose to her at "Inspiration Point," overlooking Big Creek. After their marriage, they returned many times to help us with various aspects of the ministry. He guided us through the new-computer phase and later helped with the funding and physical construction of the large log guest lodge.

Bill also served as a board member and twice as Chairman of the Board. At the critical time when Shiloh needed to pay off its debt, Bill was the man of the hour, finding and applying for the grant that would allow Shiloh to operate debt-free.

At each junction, when failure looked likely, Bill and Barbara were instruments of God's grace with encouragement and support. For all of this, we are especially grateful to God for bringing this amazing couple into our lives.

We wish God's special blessings on all that have had such a tremendous affect in helping Shiloh become what it is today.

Chapter 1

HOW IT ALL BEGAN

Saved From Disaster

I was born in 1939 in Oakland, California, during World War II. My parents were divorced when I was a toddler, so my mother, grandmother, and aunt raised me. It wasn't the normal conventional family, but it was an extremely loving and supportive one. Because my grandmother was the person who most influenced my life, she was my favorite. Although it was not a Christian home, the values taught were of a Christian nature. I never experienced the mother-father or husband-wife relationship, but I didn't know that would be a problem for me... until I was married.

Unfortunately, I married a man who had also been raised by a single mom. Neither of us had a clear picture of marriage, but we had television role models and were optimistic. After all, we'd watched *Father Knows Best,* and we believed we had the tools to make the marriage work. We also married very young and were separated by the Air Force our first three years. We honestly gave it a good try, but nine years and one child later, Bill and I divorced.

Several years later, I was introduced to Norm by a friend who believed we had much in common. That we did. We both had spouses who had left us for someone else, and we both had been left with custody of our little girls. Norm's daughter was the same age as mine. In fact, they were best friends in the day care center!

At first, I didn't want to go out with him and told my friend, "Absolutely not! I have been on too many blind dates. It's not for me; I will find my own dates. Thank you very much."

Well, he was persistent, and finally one night, he called to say that Norm had invited us all to his house for dinner and would I please reconsider. I told him I would go only if he promised to never ask me again.

The next night we arrived at Norm's home, and the first thing I noticed was that, for a single dad, he sure kept a nice clean house for himself and his daughter. I was impressed. Then, the smells coming from the kitchen really enticed me.

You have heard the saying, "The best way to a man's heart is through his stomach." Well, that works for women too, especially when it is lobster thermidor. WOW! Now I was more than impressed.

We dated for over a year, but when Norm learned he was being transferred to Minneapolis from Alameda, we decided we just weren't ready to commit to a marriage. We said our good-byes, but promised to stay in touch. And we did. We wrote each other letters and even saw each other when Norm could arrange a Navy flight to Alameda. He did this quite often—not so much to see me as to check on his house he'd rented out when he left.

One morning, as I was watching the news on television, they reported that a P2V aircraft from Twin Cities Naval Air Station had crashed on its way to Alameda. It was from Norm's squadron, and because of his habit of always trying to get that flight, I just knew he had to have been on that plane. I tried to find out from the base, but they were unable to give me any information. They had not yet notified the next of kin. Finally around

Bedtime Stories from Shiloh — Barbara Lovett

1:00 pm, my roommate suggested I try to call Norm at home. Brilliant! I anxiously dialed the number and sighed with relief when he answered. As soon as he heard my voice, he exclaimed, "No Barbara, I wasn't on that plane!" He knew right away why I was calling. He had been on duty at the base so was aware of the aircraft accident

    We talked for quite a while and finally realized we still had some very strong feelings for one another. Norm suggested I come to Minneapolis and bring my daughter, Lori, so that he and his daughter, Michele, could spend Easter together. I did, and the day before I was to return home, Norm proposed! I accepted and flew back to California the next day to quit my job, pack my things, and at last return six weeks later for the wedding! On the plane home I told Lori, and she exclaimed loud enough for the entire plane to hear, "Oh boy, my best friend is going to be my sister!" I would like to be able to say, "And they lived happily ever after," but that was not the case.

    I still did not have a clue about husband-wife relationships—not to mention blended-family relationships. But, "Never fear; TV is near!"

After all, *The Brady Bunch* seemed to have it all figured out. I soon discovered, once again, that real life was not at all like TV. To say the least, we had many difficulties in trying to put our families together.

Thankfully, Norm had been raised in a Christian home with wonderful loving parents. They had been married 65 years when his father was hit by a car and died. Norm had experienced what marriage was supposed to be like and had been raised with Christian principles. At an early age though, he decided that perhaps God was keeping him from having a good time. Consequently, for many years, he put his Christianity on the shelf.

When our marriage began falling apart, Norm decided that maybe God did know best and re-dedicated his life to Christ. He started taking us all to church every Sunday, started tithing, threw away things in our home that he perceived as "evil," and became what I considered a "Jesus Freak." Appalled, scared, and fed up, I decided I could finally understand why his first wife had left him. Little did I know, God was busily at work, saving us from certain disaster.

I called my best friend, Mary Ann, often, complaining to her about this crazy man I had married. She listened a lot but didn't say much. Unbeknownst to me, she also had become a Christian. In fact, she and Norm were both praying for me! Eventually, she invited me to a luncheon. I said, "Great! I love luncheons…sounds like fun." And I meant it. Then she proceeded to tell me (or warn me) that this was not the type of luncheon I was accustomed to; it was a Christian women's luncheon. My hopes of a fun day were dashed. After all, why in the world would I want to go to a Christian women's luncheon when I had one of "those people" living in my home? I had not been around many Christian women, but I thought I had a pretty good idea what to expect. Again, I had watched TV. I'd seen those women—the ones that wear the long black dresses, hair tucked up in a bun, no makeup, big clumsy shoes and carrying enormous black Bibles. As I hesitated, she begged and pleaded. At last I agreed to go, but only to keep her company.

As we walked into the banquet hall, I knew we had to be in the wrong place. The women were dressed beautifully—makeup and all. They looked wonderful! In fact, they had something I had never seen before: a special glow. After we ate, several of them stood up and explained why Jesus was so important in their lives. I just could not understand. They looked like they had everything a woman would want or need. Why would they need this Jesus?

Eventually, a woman stood and asked if anyone would like to have a Bible study in her home. Well, I knew that was the last thing I would ever want. God had other plans for me, though. Suddenly, I found myself raising my hand! I kept trying to pull it down, but the force was stronger than I was. As it turns out, it was during those Bible studies, in my home, that I came to know Jesus as my Lord and Savior.

I would like to say that at last we began living "happily ever after," but again that was not the case. We did begin to put our marriage under the leadership of Christ. We applied His principles for marriage, and we continued to grow in His grace. We still suffered the consequences of divorce, but we had joy unimaginable! Through the struggles, we learned so much, and eventually we used our experiences to teach others. The Lord actually eventually led us into establishing Shiloh Ranch, a very special place dedicated to strengthening and restoring the American family.

We now believe that our greatest weaknesses have become our greatest strength. We've been married over 45 years, and we operated the ranch for 25 years. We praise God for what He can do with an empty vessel willing to be used by Him.

Super Mom No More

When Norm and I married, we both gained step-daughters. The girls were best friends actually, and only seven months apart. They even looked alike, so naturally, I decided it would be fun dressing them as twins. One day a woman at the grocery store came up to me and started raving about how she just loved to see twins and how cute they were. Not wanting to tell her my whole life history, I just let her go on and on, until finally she asked the girls, "And how old are you?" Michele (my husband's daughter) promptly said, "I'm five-and-a-half and she's six." The woman immediately gave an indignant huff and stormed off. I never dressed them as twins again.

Nevertheless, I was delighted with my new family. I so wanted to be the loving mother to Michele that I felt she had never had. Her mother had divorced Norm to marry another man—a man who's interest was in building his own family; my husband had uncontested custody from the time she was about eighteen-months old. During

Bedtime Stories from Shiloh — Barbara Lovett

Michele's growing-up years, we never told her the details of why we had custody, and we never talked about the details of the divorce or criticized her mother. However, I believe children have an uncanny ability to sense things, and I believe she truly sensed a rejection from her mom. The more I tried to love her and take her mother's place, the more she rejected me.

The situation became worse when I felt her rejection and reacted to it. I couldn't understand why she wasn't happy like the rest of us. After several years of trying to be "Super Mom" to her, only to be pushed away, I gave up. I became distant and angry with her. What I didn't understand was that she had such an uncontrollable need to be loved by her real mom, that all my efforts could never make up for it. I could never replace her mom. She was grieving a tremendous loss, but I never allowed her to grieve. Instead, I just demanded she be happy. Consequently, she never got through the grieving process and ended up stuck in the anger stage. That anger continued for years and years.

If I had it to do all over, I would be the best step-mom I could be, but I would never try to force her to accept me as "Mom." I would grieve with her and comfort her, loving her unconditionally. After all, isn't that what God has done for us? He never forces us, but He accepts us into His family with all our brokenness. He comforts us as we grieve over the wreckage of our lives, and He loves us unconditionally, strengthening and restoring us unto Himself. I praise God that He can see past the anger and heal our broken hearts.

Raising Girls with Personalities

Soon after we started the ranch we began studying the four personality types according to the temperament theory: sanguine, choleric, melancholic, and phlegmatic. It was fascinating and a real eye-opener for me. I began to recognize the personalities of my children, my husband, and myself and learn how the different personality types generally interact.

I am sanguine, which means I love to have fun, I am disorganized, and sometimes words come out of my mouth without going through my brain first. I hate lapses in conversation, which usually causes me to fill in when there is a lull. I've learned this can actually be irritating for the person who has to take time to think first before uttering a word. I love to be around people—hate being alone. I am outgoing and optimistic. Sanguine folks always see the flowers where others might see the weeds.

My husband is melancholic. His temperament is almost the opposite of mine. While this can sure make life interesting at times, we have learned that this is actually good. We tend to balance each other out—unless we are trying to change the other person. Melancholies are deep thinkers, sensitive, organized, serious, and analytical. They are introverts and actually need times alone. They can also be moody and negative at times. Learning about our different personalities has helped us to not only understand each other better, but it has helped us to appreciate and admire our differences.

I am sorry I did not know about "personalities" while raising my girls. I would have done so many things differently. Lori, my oldest, was sanguine, so we were like kindred spirits. We just had fun together. Unfortunately, that was not the case with Michele, my melancholy daughter. She didn't think I was funny or cute, and when I would lose my cool with her, she would retreat to her room and pout for days. I didn't realize I had crushed her little spirit. After all, I was just angry; I didn't *mean* what I had said.

I felt very rejected when she seemed to enjoy being by herself more than being with her "fun" mother. Lori's punishment, when she misbehaved, was to restrict her to her room. She hated the isolation. Michele's, of course, was just the opposite. She had to stay in the living room with all of us.

There's no doubt, folks with sanguine and melancholic personalities definitely have different ways of looking at the same circumstances. I recall a particular time when our two little girls sure did. The apple sure doesn't fall far from the tree. Our 'adventure" began when the girls and I were driving on the freeway in San Diego during rush-hour traffic one day. Suddenly I realized I had a flat tire. I quickly pulled off the side of the road. As I got out of the van to survey the situation, I realized that it was going to be more difficult than even I had expected. Not only did I lack the ability to change a tire (Being sanguine, I always believed someone would come to my rescue), but I discovered that even if I had known how, I could not have done it. You see, we had just installed a lock on the spare tire attached to the back of the van, and being a little scatterbrained, I had actually forgotten to put that particular key on my key ring. So, there we were with a perfectly good spare tire and no way to use it. Talk about a predicament. I knew the only solution was to call my husband and have him drive the 15 miles to rescue us.

There were no cell phones back then, so the girls and I walked a few blocks to a pay phone, and I called Norm to explain our dilemma. He gave a melancholic sigh—you know the one that says, "How stupid can you be?"—but he promised he would get there as soon as traffic would allow. Then, we went back to the car to wait. As we sat there, probably looking quite distressed, 17 men stopped and offered to change the tire. I explained the situation, thanked them anyway, and they drove on.

When Norm finally arrived, the first thing our little sanguine daughter said was, "Daddy, guess what? Right in the middle of all this rush-hour traffic, 17 people stopped to offer us help. Wasn't that great?" Then Michele gave him the melancholic report, "Daddy, just think, out of all those *hundreds* of people on the freeway, *only* 17 men stopped to help us."

Being melancholic himself, Norm suggested to me, "Honey, why don't I stand here and give you the instructions on how to change a tire, so you'll have the experience to do it yourself when this happens again." As I pondered that idea, I decided very quickly that there was simply no way I was going to have everyone on that freeway gawking at me changing a tire while my husband just stood there watching. I coolly replied, "Oh no, that's alright. Now that I have the key, you can just go home, and I will wait for number 18 to come along and change it for me." He changed the tire.

God has created each of us with a unique temperament and personality. Each of these personalities has a purpose, and I now know that He wants us to be involved in accepting, loving and encouraging each other to build on our strengths and to diminish our weaknesses.

I know today that when Michele was young, she felt rejected by us because we didn't seem to understand her melancholic needs. As I think back on those days, the times she received encouragement was when she cleaned her room or performed other household chores. She always kept her room neat as a pin. I wish I had given her little silver boxes of encouragement instead of sharp criticism. If only I had understood more...

There was a time a few years ago, when I decided that God must have made a mistake in not allowing us to become parents when we were the age of grandparents. After all, we had gained so much wisdom and could do such a better job. At the age of grandparents, we could understand their personalities more clearly. God set me straight on all that, though, and had the last laugh.

When my daughter decided to move to Idaho, she asked me to take care of the grandchildren for a month while she traveled back to Chicago to move all her furniture and belongings out. Within a week I understood God's wisdom in giving children to the young. I might have had more patience and have known more parenting principles, but the reality was that I simply did not have the energy to be a full-time parent at the age of 60!

I didn't do it well when I was young, but fortunately, through the years, Michele and I have become much closer and there has been healing. When I was able to go to her, ask for her forgiveness for not understanding her, and then love and accept her as she is, the walls started to fall away. That is such a simple task in comparison to how God loves us. His love is perfect—despite all the different personalities of His kids—and I pray He helps us to love and live more like Him each day.

Chapter 2

THE SEARCH FOR SHILOH

Bedtime Stories from Shiloh — Barbara Lovett

Norm's Vision

How in the world did a girl, who was born in the San Francisco Bay Area, was raised in Oakland, and eventually lived in Chicago, Minneapolis, San Diego—all those big cities—end up six miles from Calder, Idaho? After all, back then the population was maybe 90 on a Saturday night! It really is funny where the Lord leads you.

We were not the usual Navy family. Being in the active reserves, Norm was able to be home most of his Navy career. Once a year though, he would leave for a few weeks on some kind of mission or schooling. This was the case in 1978 when he was sent to California for several weeks of training. Being away from all the hubbub of home, he had many quiet hours to contemplate his future when he would retire in 1981. His usual mode of operation was to decide what he wanted to do and then ask God to bless it. Fortunately, he had matured through the years and realized he needed to learn obedience and ask God what He wanted him to do with the rest of his life. So, in the quiet surroundings of his barracks, he spent many hours praying and asking God that exact question. "Father, what do You want me to do after I retire?" God's answer was clear.

Since becoming Christians, we made Christ the center of our marriage. We became very active in our church, working with couples who were trying to build strong marriages. Norm began reading every book he could get a hold of on marriage and teaching God's principles for marriage. During this time, our pastor mentored us and encouraged us to start a home group for people who were divorced, considering divorce, or struggling in a blended family. We also had many opportunities in our neighborhood to reach out to hurting families. We had such a burden for these families. We knew what it was like to be married, then divorced, and finally, trying to put our families back together into one blended family. Tough stuff! It was so encouraging, though, watching God take our broken marriages and use our experiences to help others avoid the same mistakes we'd made. God really did take our greatest weakness and turn them into our greatest strengths.

God's answer to Norm's prayer was plain and was pretty much like this: "Continue to do what you are doing now, except do it in a place in the Idaho wilderness, where families can come get away from all the busyness of the city and all the pressures of work, so they can focus on their relationships. Teach them the principles you've learned while around the dining room table, on a hike, canoeing or horseback riding. Build a place where they can come for a vacation with their families and have not only quality time with each other, but a spiritual experience too. Strengthen and restore families in a wilderness setting. Teach the men that by loving God more than anything else, they will be able to love their wives and their children the way God intended."

Norm was so excited to think about what God wanted him to do. Then he remembered who he was married to: Barbara, the city girl. Would she ever consent to living in the "wilderness"? So, he prayed, "God, you know my wife. I pray that if this is really from you, she will be excited when I share this vision with her. If she is not, I will know it is not from you."

In the days that followed, God kept increasing the vision. Every time Norm would pick up a magazine or book, it always seemed to have something in it about Idaho. Norm had never been to Idaho, never thought of Idaho, and hardly knew how to get to Idaho, but everything he read about it, painted it out to be the perfect place.

Finally, the time came when he was able to go back home to Chicago and share this exciting vision with his "big-city" girl. That first evening home, he sat down and began telling me what had transpired in California, how God had put it on his heart to start a Christian guest ranch—one that would really work on strengthening the American family simply through the activities we would offer at the ranch, devotions, and dinner-table talk. As he was telling the story, he could see my eyes getting bigger and bigger. He was sure I thought he was crazy. To his delight and surprise, I was quite the opposite; I was ecstatic—elated by the idea. That was the confirmation he needed to know this would be God's new direction for his life.

Over the next three years, all our vacations were a quest for such a property. That eventually led us to 80 acres of wilderness in the middle of the Idaho panhandle, where Big Creek runs into the scenic St. Joe River. It was 30 miles east of the nearest grocery store in St. Maries. At last we'd found the perfect place for us to begin our mission.

Buying Property

The nearest town was Calder, Idaho, and it was hardly more than a blip on the map, but we believed God had led us to the perfect property there, the place where we'd "retire" and begin a Christian guest ranch to strengthen families and help save marriages. As I recall, the property for sale was about 80 acres at the time, and it was owned by a little woman from Wales. Mrs. Davies' husband had died, and she wanted to move back to her homeland.

I remember vividly the day we viewed the property for the first time. It was perfect! We returned to the creek where we were camping, and we prayed about it. Surely, at last, this was it! We added up all the money we had, trying to figure out what we could actually offer as a down payment. We even added in the kids' piggy banks! Once all the figuring was done, we headed back up to the cabin and offered Mrs. Davies the amount we could pay her for the property. What we didn't know was that in Wales the buyer doesn't come down on a price. Basically, that's saying that the person selling the property is not being honest. Well, we had offered less than her asking price, so she was naturally put back. She called the realtor who told her not to worry or fret; they'd just sold the property for the price she wanted.

We were very disappointed. We wondered, "How can this be?" We'd been so sure that this was the property God wanted for us. Before we left, we told her that if something came up, and the deal fell through, to be sure to give us a call. On the way back to Chicago we pulled over next to a creek. We just sat down there and prayed, "God if this is truly what you want for our lives then we just pray that this deal will fall through, and we'll offer whatever she wants for the property in faith that you will provide it."

We were home about two days when the phone rang. It was Mrs. Davies, and she said, "Well, the deal fell through." And so of course we offered her what she wanted for the property. We didn't come close to having enough money, but it was going to be about 3 months before we would close escrow. At the end of those 3 months we still did not have enough money, but we got a call informing us that the survey on the property was wrong. They needed to do a new survey. It was October, and the surveyor was busy and couldn't get to it right away. Pretty soon the snow came. Then they had a lot of snow. It was April before they could finally get in and survey the property. By that time the Lord had provided all the money we needed for the down payment on the property. He really does have a way of working out the details. And so, our Shiloh adventure began. Little did we know just how many more details God would need to work out as we plunged ahead in faith.

Finding Affordable Horses

Nearly as soon as the ink dried on the closing contract for our ranch, we decided, "Well, now we need horses." God had set our hearts on a mission to start a Christian guest ranch. He'd led us to the perfect property along the beautiful St. Joe River in Northern Idaho and made a way for us to buy it, but we knew it wouldn't be a ranch if it didn't have horses.

A very good friend of ours, Marilyn Kruecke, called and said, "Temple Smith died a few months ago, and he owned probably over two hundred Lipizzan horses. His daughter is trying to sell some of them, because it's just too many for her to try to take care of." She'd heard the daughter was selling them for the price of horse meat, so she offered to call and inquire about the exact price.

While speaking to Mr. Smith's daughter, Marilyn explained that we were interested in buying some horses and understood the price to be quite low. The woman said, "Well, yes, we're selling them for ten-thousand a piece." Of course, that was not anywhere near the price of horse meat. My friend further explained that we were a non-profit organization and were just starting out. She ventured, "Would you by any chance be willing to donate some horses?" The woman just flat out answered, "Yes, as a matter of fact I would. How many would you like?"

Well, Marilyn about fell over! She called us up and exclaimed, "How many horses would you like? You can get them for free!" When I picked myself up off the ground, in my excitement I said, "Well let's see...maybe twenty!" Then reality set in, and I remembered that I'd have to feed them. We finally decided on four horses. They were beautiful, beautiful registered Lipizzan horses.

The next task was finding a place to board the horses. After all, we lived in Chicago, and it would be a year before we were actually moving to the ranch. Marilyn helped us with that also. She knew Mrs. Wacker, the owner of a wonderful estate there in Lake Forest, Illinois. They used to have thoroughbred horses, so she knew they had lots of stables. Being very resourceful, Marilyn called Mrs. Wacker and talked to her about the possibility of stabling our horses on the estate. Little did she know that Mrs. Wacker had gotten a similar inquiry just a week before and had flat out replied, "Oh no, I don't want any horses on my property anymore." When Marilyn asked her, explaining they were Lipizzan horses, this time Mrs. Wacker eagerly agreed, stating that she'd love to have Lipizzan horses in her pasture and barns. Another problem solved. God was again working out all the details.

When it came time for us to actually—and finally—move to Idaho, we had to figure out how in the world to get the horses there. All we had was one little truck and our car. Again, would you believe it, Marilyn had an idea. Now let me tell you, I don't know how we would have made it without her. God sure used Marilyn in a mighty way. Her husband was working at a company with two women who were very, very much horse enthusiasts. They had a big horse trailer that would hold four horses. Now they weren't Christians, and they really didn't particularly want anything to do with Christians, but when he told them about our circumstances, their response was quite enthusiastic. "Wow, we'd love to go across country and make a trip to Idaho. We've never been there!"

Well, they packed up the horses in that big trailer and made the big cross-country trip to Calder, Idaho. We were excited when they decided to stay and spend some time with us. We had many opportunities around the dinner table to share our faith with them, and I think they left with a new understanding of who Christ is and also what Christians can be like. That was another part of the move that was really special for us—another miracle on our journey. God made it clear each step of the way that getting what we had finally decided to call Shiloh Ranch was His plan, and in the end, He would always provide.

Chapter 3

GOD'S PROVISION & MIRACLES

Diving and Losing Money

Back in the 70's, when Norm was still in the Navy and stationed in San Diego, he took up the hobby of scuba diving. It was a beautiful area for diving. In those days, you could still take Abalone from the ocean, so we often dined on fish, lobster, abalone, and many other exotic treats. Our girls would come home and say, "Oh are we having Abalone AGAIN?!" They didn't appreciate it then, but now we all drool at the thought of those delectable morsels.

Norm and another friend from the Navy decided to go diving right after work one day. It was payday, so they stopped at the bank and cashed their checks on the way to the beach. Norm's habit was to put half of it in our checking account to pay the mortgage and other bills and then bring home the cash for groceries, gas and other smaller expenses.

They parked the van, put on their wetsuits, locked up the van, and preceded to the dive-spot.

After an hour of wonderful diving, they returned to the van, changed back into their civilian clothes and drove off. Both men were very hungry and thirsty so decided to stop at the Jack in the Box for a hamburger and soda. After placing their order at the drive-thru, they pulled out their wallets to pay the bill. What a surprise they had. When they opened their wallets, the cash was gone. Norm's loss was about $250, and his friend's may have been more than that. After looking the van over, they realized that one of the side windows had been jimmied open. They had been robbed. The thief had probably been watching them and knew that once they went under water they'd more than likely be gone for quite some time.

Norm returned home devastated and concerned about how we were going to make it until the next payday. Thankful that he had deposited half of his paycheck in the bank, he sat down to pay the bills. The first check he always wrote was to the Lord (his tithe). After a few minutes of debating with himself, he decided he would write out the usual amount—10% of his *full* check instead of reducing it to 10% of what he had left after being robbed. Then he wrote the other checks. Instead of paying the total amount due, he wrote the checks for half of the payment and then enclosed a letter with each one saying that in the next two months he would try and catch up. We became very frugal for those two months but were finally able to get our finances back to normal. We continued our normal tithe for both months.

Towards the end of the third month we received a check in the mail from the State of California for $250.00. We were quite surprised. We were not expecting any kind of tax refund from them and the check didn't even look like a tax refund, but what else could it be? I was going to cash it, but Norm said, "Oh, no. Don't cash it yet. I don't want to have the state coming back next year saying we owe them this money because it was a mistake." He asked me to call them first to find out what the check was for. I agreed, and I called first thing the next morning. I explained to the woman how we'd received a check and had no idea why we had received it and how we really wanted to know before we cashed it. She asked for the serial number of the check, the amount, and who it was payable to. After giving her all the information she promised to call the next day after she'd had a chance to look into it.

The next day she called and said, "Mrs. Lovett, I am sorry. I have searched all of our records, and I find no such serial number or anything showing that we have sent you that check."

"Well, what should I do? Is it OK to cash the check? Where in the world could it have come from?" I asked.

"Yes, go ahead and cash the check. I have no idea why you received it, and we have NO record of issuing it. It looks like a gift from heaven, to me!"

When she said she thought it was a gift from heaven, I could hardly speak. I wondered if it really could be—whether it was truly a miracle. Well, I decided it was, and I cashed the check. That was in the 70's, and no one has ever called to say they made a mistake. I'm still amazed that it was the exact amount that was stolen from Norm's wallet. When I get to heaven, I will be excited to hear exactly how God did that.

Since I was a young teenager, I have always considered my finances to be like a Yo-Yo; sometimes they are up, and sometimes they are down. The truth I have learned from that is, it doesn't matter. What is important is whether I'm being a good steward of what God has given me. Very soon after I became a Christian, I realized the joy I could receive in being a faithful giver of what God has entrusted to me. That was quite a change from how I thought about tithing when Norm first dedicated his life to Christ and started "giving away" the money I wanted for a car. Through the years, God has sure developed my joyful giving in some miraculous and even comical ways.

Amigo

I've learned through the years that miracles often arrive at the last minute and in the bleakest of circumstances, yet God has always provided. One time at Shiloh, we realized that we needed about fifteen-hundred dollars. We didn't know how we were going to get it, so we began reviewing our assets. As we looked out at the pasture, it dawned on us that right there were some of our most valuable assets. So, it was decided that we should try to sell one of the horses to pay this bill.

Our best horse, Amigo, was a beautiful white Lipizzan born right there at the ranch—our first foal. That made him extremely precious to us, of course. Not only was he our most valuable horse, but he was probably more loved than any of the other horses. As we put the word out, we got a call from a man on the east coast who was really interested in buying this horse, and he was willing to pay us ten-thousand dollars! He said he'd send us a check for $3,000.00 right away and then send someone with a horse-trailer to pick up the horse and pay the balance. It all sounded just wonderful—except losing Amigo.

The day we received the $3,000 deposit, we brought the horse in from the pasture and noticed that the fluid in one of his eyes was completely grey. We called the vet immediately. He came out and, after examining Amigo, told us that, unfortunately, the horse had a very serious ½ inch cut to his cornea (probably from some barbwire). Ointment would have to be applied to his eye every two hours for about a month. There was no guarantee, but we would just have to hope that it would heal.

Naturally, we called the man who wanted to buy the horse and explained the situation to him. He said, "Well, I really want the horse, so let's just see what happens. We'll wait the month till the end of the treatment, and then I'll make a decision based on the vet's report. Either way, you can keep the $3,000 deposit." Our job was now cut out for us. Thank goodness for the wonderful and dedicated ranch hands.

Bill Stauber was our main ranch hand, and Kathy Ahrens was our help in the kitchen. Kathy was also a nurse by trade, so she volunteered to help Norm and Bill with Amigo's treatments. They all took shifts during the night, waking Amigo up and putting the ointment in his eye. The horse got so used to it that sometimes he wouldn't even get up while they treated him. You can be assured, though, that the ones applying the ointment were wide awake and very sleep-deprived. It was a long and laborious task, but at the end of the month, the reward for all the hard work was a celebration. The vet declared Amigo's eye was completely healed—no scar.

We immediately called the buyer on the east coast with the good news. He was delighted that the horse was fine, but he informed us that he had gotten anxious and had purchased another horse. He no longer needed Amigo, but because of the agreement he had made, he said he really wanted us to keep the $3,000.

God sure used our "bad circumstances" for good! Because of that cut in Amigo's eye, we ended up with the money we needed (actually more than we needed) *and* were able to keep our most valuable and loved horse. He lived a long life (over 25 years) and was such a delight to everyone who rode him. His name Amigo ("Friend" in Spanish) surely fit his personality. That wasn't the first time God had used our "bad circumstances" for good, and it wouldn't be our last. Sometimes it wasn't until years later that I was able to see the good in it, though.

The Concrete Miracle

We experienced many miracles at Shiloh. I recall one day when we had a counseling appointment with a woman who had been really struggling in a marriage to a very abusive husband. She finally decided she needed to separate, but she was just so afraid to leave. A major issue for her was not being able to trust that God would indeed take care of her needs. Well, before her appointment that day, we got a call letting us know the time the concrete truck would arrive to pour the concrete for a water cistern we were building. Knowing her appointment was at noon, Norm did a little calculating and said, "I think we can get that done in time. Come on up."

When the truck arrived, they headed up the steep hill where we needed the concrete poured. Soon we realized there was a problem, though. The road was so narrow that the driver couldn't get the truck all the way up to the area where we needed to pour. We had a couple of boys working with us at the time, so they ended up having to move the concrete in wheelbarrows to the pour site. As you can imagine, it took a lot longer for the concrete project to get done, and Norm was really getting concerned about making our counseling session.

Norm finally came down the hill and explained, "I'm sorry we're going to be a little late. We've got to get this concrete poured or it'll just dry in the truck." The woman was very understanding, so the men finished up the project.

When the driver finally explained that he was going to have to charge a lot more because of the overtime, I couldn't help but be concerned. We had put aside money for the concrete; we had a pretty good idea how much it would cost. We always paid cash for everything, and we thought we had put enough money aside, but we hadn't accounted for all the extra time. "Oh my gosh! How are we going to pay for this concrete?" I fretted. So, this woman and I sat down and prayed about it.

We prayed that somehow God would provide the money for the concrete. After all, we couldn't return concrete! Not long after we prayed, the doorbell rang. It was our neighbor; she'd just been to the post office. Now, she'd never done this before, but she had decided to pick up our mail for us. When I went through the mail, I noticed right away that there were some checks for the ranch. I added them up. I don't remember *exactly* how much they totaled, but I remember very distinctly that it was exactly the extra amount we needed for the concrete! When the concrete man came down and told us how much it was all going to cost, I looked at what we'd just received in the mail and what we'd already set aside, and I knew that God had truly provided just what we needed. *That* was a miracle, but the best part of that miracle was how the woman responded to what she'd seen God do for us. She exclaimed, "Oh my gosh! If YOU can trust God for THAT, then I KNOW I can trust God, too. I see that God is faithful, and I'm going to trust Him to meet MY needs."

That's The Ticket

If you've ever read the book *The Hiding Place*, then you know it's the story of Corrie Ten Boom, and you might remember how her father sat down with her one day and explained that you never get the train ticket until you get to the train station. That was his way of explaining that God doesn't meet our need until it is a need. Well, that little lesson really touched my heart. As a matter of fact, it became a principle for my life. Whenever we had a need, I would always remember that and look to God to meet it at just the right time.

One time when we had some boys working at the ranch, we were sitting around the table after devotions together and I told them, "Boys, today when we pray, we really need to pray that God would meet our need. We have a bill for $120.00, and we don't have the money. We need to pray that God would provide that. I'm going to the post office at noon to pick up the mail, so let's pray." For me, the post office was the train station, and a check in the mail was the ticket. So, we prayed, and later on I went down to the post office. I picked up the mail and started going through it. Sure enough, there were some checks there. When I added them all up, there was $125.00! I thought, "Oh my gosh! God has truly met our need—even went over and above!"

The first thing the boys said when they came in that evening was, "Did you get the ticket? Did you get the ticket?" I told them that not only did we get the ticket but we got $5.00 more than we'd needed. Later on when I began going through the rest of the mail, I opened up my bank statement and noticed I had a $5.00 service charge. I said, "Wow, He gave us a ticket when I didn't even know I needed it! Isn't God good; He's so faithful to meet our needs!"

The Player Piano & Washing Machine

Have you ever had something in your home that was truly a treasure to you? Maybe an antique your grandmother left to you, some wonderful bargain you found at a garage sale, or perhaps a gift someone special gave you? One day at one of the women's retreats, I was asked, "What is your favorite thing in the lodge?" I didn't even have to think about it. Picturing my special treasure, I said, "My player piano." I hadn't always been such a fan of pianos, though.

When I was a young girl, we had a piano in our home. My mom made sure that I had piano lessons and singing lessons. At first I enjoyed them both and had many opportunities to sing in public. Then my mom said that if I practiced really, really hard, and gave up most of my social life, I might one day become a professional singer and piano player, able to support my family. Well first of all, even as a child, I had a sanguine personality. My social life was extremely important to me. Secondly, when I thought about my future, my desire was to get married and be a wife and mother, not work to support my family. So, her comment did not motivate me to practice. Eventually she gave up and sold the piano.

Years later, when the pressure was gone to play or sing, I found enjoyment in them again. Whenever I found an opportunity to stand around a piano singing, that's where I would be. There just weren't that many opportunities to do that, though, unless I wanted to go to a piano bar. Since becoming a Christian, bars were not exactly on my list of places to spend my time. But I have a thoughtful husband who knew me well, and he found a way to fulfill my desire. He purchased a wonderful old 1918 Lester Player Piano that had just been completely reconditioned. It even came with 50 piano rolls! It was absolutely a dream come true. That piano brought so much joy to our home. What fun we had sitting around singing and dancing to all of those great old piano rolls.

As time went by, one day when I was just getting ready to leave the church where I worked as the pastor's secretary, I received an urgent call from my daughter: "Mom, quick come home! The basement's flooded..." I jumped in my car and sped the 10 miles to our home. Norm was stationed with the Navy in Glenview at the time, so we lived in base housing—in a fourplex—at the Great Lakes Naval Training Station. As I drove up to the house, I could see that things were not good. All the neighbors were out running from door to door with buckets, mops, towels—anything that could be used to extract water. All four apartments in our building were indeed flooded. A huge water tank behind our building had broken, and all of the water was pouring into our basements. Walking down the basement stairs, my heart sank. There sat at least two feet of water from wall to wall.

When we moved into our home, the Navy allowed us to partition our basement into additional rooms, so we had a laundry room, a family room, and an office for Norm—now all under 2 feet of water. I remember a 20-pound bag of dog food had spilled out and the soggy kibbles were floating on top of the water. What a mess! Taking a quick inventory, I noticed the water was almost up to the keyboard of our beloved player piano. Our washing machine and dryer were 2 feet under. Everything lower than 24 inches in Norm's office was soaked, including his prized stamp collection from his teenage years.

Somehow our church heard the news, and within an hour many of our church family arrived to help not only us, but our neighbors, too. It was quite a witness, especially to our next door neighbor. She had frantically called her husband at work, but he said he was too busy and she'd just have to clean it up herself. Well, she was so angry she decided to just open a bottle of bourbon, sit, and wait for him to come home. Needless to say, our friends were a real God-send to her. It took many man hours, but finally we were able to get all of the water out.

The next day the Navy sent their inspectors out to get an estimate of the damage. We were told to call a professional piano tuner for a repair estimate, take our stamp collection to a collector for an appraisal of the ruined stamps, and call

Sears to look at our washing machine and dryer for the repair costs.

The piano repairman specialized in player pianos and informed us that, because the piano was an antique, it had been put together with animal glue, which dissolves in water. He said it would take a few months, but eventually the piano would just fall apart. Also, he said the soundboard would eventually rust. I was heartsick. My wonderful piano that I loved so much... The estimate for the damage was the total value of the piano, $2,000.

We took the stamp books to a collector, and while we might not have been able to sell the stamps for their true value, that's the value he had to use for the appraisal.
Sears came out and told us that the motors in both machines would need to be replaced; they were expected to rust out. All the estimates were sent to the Navy for their consideration.

Meanwhile, it was time for what would be our final vacation to Idaho, looking for land where we would start our Christian guest ranch, so we packed up and headed west. That was the year we found the property near Calder.

Several weeks after arriving back in Illinois, we received a very large check from the Navy for all the damages caused by the flood. Looking at the check, the first thing Norm said was, "Barb, I know how much you love that piano, but I really think we shouldn't use this money to buy another one or have this one repaired. Let's use it for starting the ranch. We can take the piano with us and just wait for it to fall apart. At least you might have a few months left to play it. Also, the washing machine and dryer are still working, so let's just wait till they quit, too." I agreed; I knew we really did need that money to start the ministry. I also knew I would grieve the loss of that special piano.

Ten years later, would you believe, that piano was still working just fine?! Somehow that animal glue never did dissolve. I did decide that perhaps after moving it several times it might need to be tuned, though. At least that was what I'd always heard. I knew a man in our church was a piano tuner, so I called and invited him to the ranch to take a look at the piano. After playing the piano, his first remark was, "Did you get this piano tuned lately? It sure doesn't need to be tuned at this point in time." When I gave him the full history of that piano, he was astounded. Matter of fact, he said, "That truly is a miracle piano."

It has now been well over 30 years since "The Chicago Flood," and that piano still fills our home with such beautiful music and keeps me dancing. God really cares about the delight of our lives. But that wasn't the only miracle to come out of that flood.

After moving to Idaho, we continued using the washing machine and dryer. They really got a work-out, too, with all the guests' needs, sheets, towels, and our personal laundry. Then when we had the MMAPERS (Mobile Missionary Assistant Persons) at the ranch helping us build during the summer months, the washer and dryer were literally being used all day long every day.

One day our dryer stopped working, so I called Sears to come out and repair it. While he was there I asked him to check the washing machine, too. The dryer just needed a new belt, and the washing machine was fine. Mind you, these were the same old motors from the flood. As the repairman was writing out the bill, he remarked, "Wow! I looked at the serial numbers on these machines. I know how old they are, but they are like brand new! You must not use them very much." I could only stare at him in unbelief. "Use them?" I replied, "Heavens, they hardly ever stop being used."

Years later we experienced another flood. Except this time it was in the lodge at the ranch. We had 3,000 gallons of hot water flood two of the bedrooms upstairs, which eventually caused the floors to collapse. The water ended up in the downstairs area. I immediately ran down to the recreation room, where our player piano was. I was amazed to discover that, while the water had flooded towards the piano, it had stopped just a few feet from it! At midnight, as all the workers were leaving from cleaning up, I decided to make sure the piano was still working. I grabbed a piano roll without looking at the title and started to play. The song was "Piano Roll Blues." The words rang out, "I wanna hear it again. I wanna hear it again – the old piano roll blues." *Amazing* is the only word I could think of at that time. God did it again, another miracle. I am still in awe at how God can use those bad times in our lives for something good. I never dreamed our piano and washing machine would have such a role in purchasing Shiloh Ranch...or strengthening my faith.

Bedtime Stories from Shiloh — Barbara Lovett

Up Close and Personal

It was fall, and hunting season was upon us. It was time for Norm to fully concentrate on harvesting an elk. Idaho has a terrible habit of always scheduling the opening day of elk season on my birthday, and that year was no different. I sulked all morning about what a lonely birthday it was going to be—no cake, no present, no singing, not even one person to help me celebrate. Anyone who knows me knows how much I love parties. It was a woe-is-me morning. I had forgotten what a wonderful and loving Father I have.

Interrupting my pity party, a truck came up our driveway mid-morning. It was Jim, the owner of the local saw mill. I had contacted him many times over the previous weeks, trying to get - lumber chips from his mill to use in the horse stalls. They are wonderful for keeping the stalls dry and sweet smelling. Okay, maybe "sweet" is a bit exaggerated, but they did make the smell tolerable. We'd gone without for over a month because he wasn't able to load the chips into our truck; his front-end loader was broken. Our only other option was to load the chips by hand, or rather, shovel. It would have taken days. Jim, of course, was unwilling to do that, and I really didn't have the strength or desire to attempt it. I'm sure that if the horses were capable of doing it themselves, they would have though. They didn't enjoy their dirty, smelly, wet stalls either.

Besides doing all the cooking, house cleaning, secretarial work, entertaining of houseguests, and various other household jobs, in those early days at the ranch, I also took on the task of mucking out the stalls. Oh, what I would have given for a pile of those wonderful chips. They made the job so much easier, and it was a lot more satisfying when it was done. All this is to say, I was certainly curious and a little excited to see Jim at my door.

After cordial greetings between us, his purpose became clear. "Well, guess what Barbara? I finally got my front-end loader working, and if you would like to have Norm bring your big dump truck down to the mill, I'll load it with the chips you need."

I was about to jump for joy until I remembered that I didn't even know how to drive that huge truck, let alone operate the dump feature. "Gosh Jim, I think we are going to be out of luck if you need it moved in the next couple of days. Norm is out on a hunting trip, and I don't expect him back till the weekend. Can you wait till then?"

Clearly disappointed, he replied, "Oh, Barb, I'm sorry, I need to get it moved today."

Before really thinking, I kidded, "Wow that would have been a great birthday present."

It was his turn to be curious. He asked, "Whose birthday is it?" Well, when I told him it was mine, he thoughtfully countered, "Okay, wait a minute. If you would allow me to drive your truck, I will load it for you and bring it back. Consider it my birthday present to you".

I burst out, "Oh my gosh! That would be wonderful. Of course, you can drive our truck!" I grabbed the keys and off he went. An hour later he returned with the truck loaded to the brim with those wonderful chips. And that wasn't the end—he made 3 trips! When he was done, I had a mountain of chips that would last for months. What a beautiful birthday present! I thanked Jim, but I thanked God most. I knew it was His perfect timing and really His very personal gift to me.

When Norm came home several days later with a bounty of elk meat, he immediately lamented, "Barb, I feel so bad that I wasn't home for your birthday. I hope it ended up at least being a pleasant day."

I could hardly contain my excitement. "Norm, not only was it a pleasant day, but Jesus celebrated with me and gave me a wonderful birthday present. Come with me, and I'll show you!" Of course he was shocked and amazed when he saw the mountain of chips and wondered how in the world I had managed it. After a full explanation, I laughed and pointed out, "The Bible says that God can move mountains. For my birthday He moved a mountain of chips!"

That experience was such an up-close and personal one for me. It showed me that even when I was being selfish and self-centered, God was still willing to care for and love me. Time and time again, I continue to realize just how personal God can be with us, and how He really does care about every hair on my head.

The Miracle of the Canada Geese

There's a reason why Shiloh Ranch was amply decorated with Canada geese. Well, maybe more than one, but they have special significance to Norm and I.

Through the years at Shiloh, many visitors have heard the devotion concerning the character qualities of the Canada geese. Using the Scripture, 2 Timothy 2:22-26, Norm would correlate the difference between the goose and the seagull, then applying it to our lives and showing us how we should be an encouragement to those around us. The devotion went something like this:

After courting, the goose and gander pair off and become lifetime mates. Any approaching rival will probably be driven away by both geese. They also have a strong reliance on and loyalty to the community from which they gain support and encouragement. They are so loyal to one another that if one is injured, the whole group may delay their departure until that member is strong enough.

Bedtime Stories from Shiloh   Barbara Lovett

In their long-range spring and fall migrations, they fly in a "V" formation. The goose in the lead provides the leadership and navigation guidance for the entire flock. Due to the stress of this leadership, the leader changes every thirty minutes. They fly in this formation even in the black of night at high altitude.

Ever hear them honking? Scientists believe they encourage each other by their honking. They might be saying things like: "You can do it." "Keep it up!" "We're behind you." "We're in this together." Studies have shown that they can fly 60 % further as a group than individually, and this is believed to be due to the encouragement they are to each other.

On the other hand, have you ever watched the seagulls at the ocean? They are great solo flyers, beautiful acrobats, but they go it alone. As a group they are greedy and quarrelsome. They fight over fish and scold each other. They are unruly, squabbling, noisy, disorganized, selfish, and petty. Worst of all, they steal from one another.

We all have seagull natures before we are saved. It is God's salvation and His spirit within us that makes it possible for us to have new natures like the Canada goose. We need more Christians like the Canada geese and fewer Christians who behave like the seagulls. We need to be encouragers of one another. In other words – we need to "HONK" at each other.

Norm's translation to the scripture goes like this:

"Flee the evil desires of the seagulls and pursue righteousness, faith, love and peace, along with the other Canada geese who call on the Lord out of a pure heart. Don't have anything to do with the foolish and stupid arguments of the seagulls, because you know they produce quarrels. And the Lord's Canada geese must not quarrel; instead he must be kind to everyone, even the seagulls, able to teach, not resentful. Those seagulls who oppose him, he must gently instruct, in the hope that God will grant them repentance leading them to a knowledge of the truth, and that they will come to their senses and escape from the trap of the head seagull, who has taken them captive to do his will."

It's true, Canada geese are amazing and beautiful creatures, and we can learn many lessons from their devotion and loyalty, but God used them to encourage us in a very special way one day. We were at an all-time low, and were preparing to leave Shiloh Ranch and "give up." As we were making plans to leave, we heard the faint sound of honking. Walking outside, we saw a flock of Canada geese in their usual "V" formation, coming over the mountains toward our cabin. Because it wasn't their usual migrating time, we were a bit surprised and curious. As they reached the cabin, they broke formation and started circling above the cabin, honking incessantly. After several minutes, they regrouped into formation and flew back the same way they had come. Norm and I just stood there in amazement! It was as if they had come on a special mission to our cabin—to honk encouragement to us!

We knew it was God speaking to us, encouraging us to stay and continue the ministry. And stay we did. Over the years, we shared this story and our fondness for the Canada geese with many visitors. To this day, watching these geese, we see a wonderful example of God's love and the power of encouragement.

Chapter 4

GOD'S PEOPLE

God's Merciful Healing

In 1995, Norm and I traveled around the United States showing a professional video that had been made about Shiloh Ranch. During those travels, we decided to stop off in Sacramento and have dinner with Bill, my ex-husband. We had remained friends after the divorce, and he tried to keep a good relationship with our daughter, also. Unfortunately, he had never found marital happiness. After our divorce, he married a wonderful lady, also named Barbara. They had a son, and it seemed for a while that things were going well. After about 4 years, though, that marriage also fell apart. Bill was married five times before he finally gave up his search for that "made in heaven marriage." Lori prayed fervently for her father through those years, and finally, when he was in his 50's, her prayers were answered. Bill became a Christian and began trusting his life to the Lord.

On the return leg of our trip, we made arrangements to meet with Bill at a local cafe. We waited and waited, and finally Norm turned to me and said, "Isn't that Bill over there?" I looked at this man who looked to be at least 10 years older than Bill. He was very drawn, thin, and almost emaciated. It didn't look like the handsome man I had known. But when I looked closer, I recognized his expressive eyes. Yes, that was indeed Bill, but something was very wrong.

We talked for a bit with him, but he didn't explain his deteriorating appearance. I surely didn't want to say, "Wow, do you look awful." I decided it would be better if Lori called to inquire. She did, and to our dismay, she discovered that he had cancer. Actually, he didn't even know it until Lori called and suggested, or rather, demanded that he go to a doctor. In the next two months his health deteriorated so fast that he was unable to work or even care for himself. I will be forever grateful to my husband, Norm, for both the financial and emotional support he graciously provided to Bill during that time.

Three months after Bill's diagnosis, Lori received the call that he was in the hospital. He wasn't expected to live through the weekend. Lori had just had a baby. Born premature, the baby would have to stay in the hospital, but Lori was being released. She asked if I would go with her to Sacramento to see her dad, make all the arrangements, and take care of cleaning out his apartment. There were so many other details that had to be done, and she could only be away for 3 days. I knew she needed some emotional support, too.

When Lori and I arrived at the airport, Barbara, Bill's second wife, met us. She and Lori had stayed close over the years, as she had been a wonderful step-mom. Immediately making her intentions known, she exclaimed, "I will help the two of you in any way I can, but do not ask me to help Bill. He ruined my life, and I want no part of him."

She drove us to Bill's apartment where we picked up his car and went to the hospital. We were told the room he was in, but when we walked in and saw the man lying in the bed, we felt there must be some mistake. It just couldn't be Bill. He looked like an 80-year-old man just out of a concentration camp! When he opened his eyes, though, I knew it was him.

He saw me standing there and tried to speak. I put my ear up close to his mouth, so that I could hear him, and he asked, "What are you doing here?"

I responded, "Oh Bill, didn't you know I'd come? After all, you were my first love." Tears welled up in his eyes.

He seemed to draw some strength and comfort from seeing Lori and I, and after a few hours was able to talk more. At one point he said, "You know Barb, it wasn't your fault. You didn't do anything to cause the divorce; it was me. I just want you to know that I always loved you. I loved you when I divorced you, and I continued to love you through the years. I am so sorry for all the pain I have caused in so many lives." He went on to explain that he was actually glad we divorced, because he would have ruined my life. I would have never found Norm, and I might never have found God. He said Norm was the best father Lori could have ever had…and could I please tell him how much he loved and appreciated him for all he had done for both of us.

He concluded, "So, all in all, it turned out for the best. But I am still so very sorry for the hurt I caused my second wife, Barbara. I ruined her life." I can't fully describe the healing that came with his words.

After we left the hospital that day, we met Barbara for dinner. I told her about our conversation with Bill and specifically what he had remorsefully confessed concerning her. She sighed deeply and said, "Oh-my-gosh. He's finally admitted that he ruined my life; he finally realizes the hurt he caused me. Please tell him that I forgive him." After dinner, back at the hospital with Bill, we shared what Barbara had said. It was such an encouragement to him. It seemed to really perk him up, too. In fact, a short time later, a couple we'd been friends with when we were married showed up, and Bill was able to sit up, joke, and laugh with them until they left about an hour and a half later! He sure wasn't carrying on like a man who was dying.

As we were getting ready to leave the hospital, I mentioned that Lori needed him to sign a form to sell his car. Startled, he responded, "Oh no. Don't sell my car; I'm going to need it. I'm going to get well. Matter of fact, I don't think there was anything wrong with me except the stress of my financial burdens and the weight of guilt I've felt for all I had done to you and Barbara. But you have taken care of all that. I feel forgiven. The burden has been lifted, and I know I am going to get well." I was at a loss for words, as the doctor had told me just the night before that he only had 34 percent of his heart working…and he would not make it through the weekend.

In the morning when we arrived back at the hospital, I was greeted by the doctor again. He now informed me that Bill had improved so much that he would have to be transferred to a convalescent hospital. "Wow," I thought, "maybe Bill was right!" I was amazed at what effect the emotions have on the body…and forgiveness. We made arrangements to admit him to a nursing care facility. The hospital even insisted that he didn't need an ambulance or a nurse; we could drive him there ourselves. It was absolutely a miracle. But God was just getting started! Two hours after we got Bill settled, Barbara came to the facility, visited with him, and then assured Lori and me that she would now be responsible for his care. What tremendous healing was at work!

The next day we flew home, confident that he would be well taken care of. We hardly needed a plane; we were already flying so high. Our joy was tremendous. I couldn't wait to get home to share all that had happened with Norm. Of course, he was delighted, and we rejoiced together over the changed hearts.

Three days later, we received the call that Bill had gone home to be with the Lord. I thank God for the opportunity God had given me. It was such a privilege to be a part of His merciful process of forgiveness and restoration...even at that "last hour." We delight in knowing that Bill left this earth with a renewed spirit and void of all those burdens of guilt. His body had withered away, but his heart was healed!

A Shower or Ministry?

It has been said that some of our greatest memories come from those times in our lives when we've experienced adversity or hardships. That theory really bore out during those first 10 years at Shiloh while we were trying to build the facilities.

We were not known for our beautiful and comfortable accommodations during that time. We had many groups come from all over the United States, and the best we had for them was the loft of the barn. If you like the smell of manure (which surprisingly, I've learned, some do) or the smell of hay and horses, you might have enjoyed the loft. It was actually divided by large tarps—guys on one side and ladies on the other. There were no soft comfortable mattresses; instead, guests slept on air mattresses with sleeping bags. It was definitely a camping-out atmosphere. Meals were served open-air on picnic tables in the front yard. I cooked for 10 to 20 people on a little four burner stove in a kitchen that could accommodate one cook at a time. Norm and I lived in the little cabin on the property. It had one guest bedroom which was usually occupied by the visiting group's leader.

Getting a shower could be a real challenge, especially for Norm, since there was just one bathroom. He was committed to making sure it was always available for a guest. Consequently, his time for the bathroom was usually around four in the morning, before any of the guests stirred. We did have one guest, though, who was also an early riser. He'd venture down to the cabin each morning for his quiet time and to start the coffee for everyone. On these days, Norm felt a little competition for his alone time in the bathroom.

One morning there came a knock at the front door as Norm was enjoying his hot shower and our early riser, Brian, was in the kitchen reading his Bible. Brian discovered a determined young woman before him when he opened the door. She greeted him and quickly explained that she'd noticed the ranch sign at the bottom of the driveway and wanted to rent a horse. Surprised by the request, especially at four in the morning,

Brian hesitated, "Just a moment...I'm just a guest here, but I'll get the owner." He closed the door and headed to the bathroom.

Knocking, he asked, "Norm can you come out? There is a lady here who'd like to rent a horse."

Norm was a bit shocked but amused by the clever way Brian was trying to push him out of the bathroom. He said, "Oh Brian, come on. I'll be out in a few minutes, and then you can have the bathroom."

Brian laughed and said, "No, really Norm. There's a lady here who wants to rent a horse."

Impressed, Norm responded, "Brian, it is four in the morning. You can't really expect me to believe there's someone here to rent a horse... but I have to admit that you have a unique way of trying to get me out of the bathroom. You must really be in a hurry today."

Brian glanced back towards the front hall, not sure how to convince Norm. He urged again,

"Please Norm, come and see for yourself. I'm telling the truth."

At last Norm agreed to come out, but let Brian know it was only because of his ingenuity and persistence. He dried himself off, threw on his jeans and shirt and headed to the front door.

Sure enough, just as Brian had said, there certainly was a young woman waiting for him...at four in the morning. "Can I help you?" he asked.

"Yes, I saw that you had horses, and I would really like to rent one," she replied. She seemed quite determined.

Still very surprised that anyone would be standing at the door wanting to rent a horse at four in the morning, Norm said, "I'm sorry we don't rent horses; they are only used for the guests staying here. We are a Christian guest ranch. We work with couples and families to strengthen and restore marriages." He grabbed a brochure off the hall table and handed it to her.

This time it was the woman's turn to be shocked. Accepting the brochure, her shoulders drooped, and she almost immediately started to cry. Finally, she confessed, "Actually, *this* is exactly what I need." Then she began to explain the reason she wanted to rent a horse. She was just sure her husband was camped up at Big Creek with another woman, and she wanted to ride up on a horse "like Lady Godiva" and catch him in the act.

At this point, Norm knew this was not an accident but an opportunity from God to minister to this grieving lady. To keep from waking any of the others, he stepped outside and guided her to the picnic table where they could talk more in-depth. Around six I got up to start cooking breakfast. Brian was still in the cabin drinking his coffee. I looked out the window and immediately noticed Norm and a woman I had never seen before sitting at the picnic table in what appeared to be a pretty heavy conversation. A bit surprised, I asked Brian, "What is Norm doing out there, and who is he is talking to?"

Brian told me the remarkable story, and we decided this was an important time for us to pray for her. Pretty soon all the guests were up, coming into the cabin with puzzled looks on their faces and wondering the same thing as me. We briefly explained, and they all decided to join us in prayer.

That wonderful and unusual morning, the woman accepted Jesus as her Savior. She and Norm continued to talk until almost 9:00. Norm finally told her that he really had to go; he needed to take the group to Avery where they would lead a Vacation Bible School for the children in that community. She decided to drive her car up to Big Creek. She wanted to bring her husband back to the ranch for some marriage counseling.

True to her word, they both returned in the afternoon, but it was obvious he didn't really want to be there. He was fighting mad. Norm and I decided they needed to be separated for a few hours, so I took her in the cabin with me while Norm talked with him outside. Just for the record, this young man was not camped out with another woman, but rather, he was on an assignment with the Forest Service. She'd found him alone in his camper.

That day, both of them became Christians and became our good friends. In fact, he served as Chairman of the Board for Shiloh many years later, and we became Godparents for their son. God had a plan that day many years ago, and that memory will always remain as one of the best days at Shiloh...even if we did only have one bathroom.

The Beauty of a Butterfly

Each summer at Shiloh Ranch, teenagers who were interested in learning certain skills or good work ethics would come to stay. Usually, they also wanted to grow in their spiritual life and develop a closer walk with God. It was exciting watching them mature in so many different ways. Occasionally, we'd have some who, after several days on the job, would decide that the work was just too hard for them. After all, mucking horse stalls and bucking hay were not the easiest tasks in the world—especially if you were from the city where taking out the garbage was the most strenuous job you had ever done. When they were about ready to hang up the towel and head for an easier life, I would tell them a story that I believe really encouraged them to "keep on keeping on." And so it goes....

Years ago, there was a man who studied butterflies. What really fascinated him was their transformation from worm to butterfly via the cocoon. He was especially intrigued, perhaps a bit disturbed, by their prolonged struggle to emerge.

Painstakingly, they would chew, tear, and wrestle, trying to force the ultimate release. He began contemplating what would happen if he could release them before they had to go through the struggle. He finally decided to use a sharp knife and slit the enclosure lengthwise, allowing the insect to emerge freely without the struggle. And what happened next completely changed his outlook. They all emerged easily enough, but without the beautiful luster or color he had come to expect. Their wings were very wet, and they couldn't fly. They were lethargic and weak. Eventually, they all died. He concluded from this experiment that it is the struggle within the cocoon that is absolutely essential to the proper development and even survival of the butterfly.

So too, it is for the Christian. In fact, life's pressures can produce positive, wonderful results. The harder the trial or test of life, the greater the possibility of real growth or change for better, if handled correctly. God uses the difficulties in our life to develop our character, strength, and beauty. We mustn't pray for an easy life, but rather, that God would give us what we need to persevere, wrestling through the tough times. I can praise Him in the storms, because I know, that like the butterfly, God is making me beautiful. I believe that story made a difference in the lives of some of those teenagers, too.

The adventure begins! May 8, 1969.

Arial view of our property in the wilderness, 1981.

The original cabin.

Bill Westrate, Chairman of the Board.

Amigo.

Celebration time... The lodge is finished!

A teaching moment.

Where most of the ministry took place...
Around the dining room table.

Chapter 5

THE ANGELS THAT

GOT HAZARDOUS DUTY PAY

Bedtime Stories from Shiloh — Barbara Lovett

Kicked by a Horse

When Norm was in the Navy, he got "Hazardous Duty" pay for some of his assignments. At Shiloh Ranch, there was no "Hazardous Duty" pay for Norm, but soon after we moved in, we were pretty certain he had a guardian angel who deserved it.

One of those "close calls" happened soon after one of our wonderful horses died. We decided we needed to buy another horse, and although we had always had Lipizzans or Paso Vinos, Norm thought it was time to try a different breed. Morgans had always interested him, so he proceeded to search for just the right one. After several months, he finally saw an ad for a Morgan stallion. After a call to the owner, and discovering he was still for sale, we drove to their ranch just on the outskirts of Sandpoint.

The horse was out in a pasture by himself, but in the next pasture was a beautiful mare. There was no gate on the pasture so we had to climb under the barbwire fence to get to him. The owner walked up to the horse, put the halter on him, and then walked the horse over to Norm. At this point the horse seemed a little jumpy around Norm, so he stood back a few feet from the stallion. But that just wouldn't do. He was so edgy about Norm that the horse immediately took one big jump and kicked Norm with his two back feet directly on Norm's chest. Norm flew in the air and landed right next to the fence. As Norm looked over at the horse, he saw the stallion coming at him fast, with the intention of kicking him again, he was sure. Norm quickly dove under the fence for safety and then doubled over in pain.

I ran for the car and drove up as close to Norm as I could. With the help of the owner, we were able to get him in the car, and after getting directions to the nearest hospital, I sped off. I was sure Norm had some broken ribs, but I thought that was probably the extent of his injuries.

Once Norm was admitted into the ER, it seemed like an eternity before the doctor finally came out. He said, "Mrs. Lovett, I am sorry but I am afraid Norm has had some life-threatening injuries, and we are going to have to fly him to Spokane. His liver has been cut and he has internal bleeding."

I was shocked. I had no idea it was so serious. Immediately, I called my daughter, Lori, and the church asking for prayer. Lori said she and her husband would drive from Coeur d'Alene and meet me in an hour or so. We decided Lori would drive me to the hospital in Spokane, and her husband would drive my car back home. Unfortunately, while we were at the hospital, it had started to snow hard. A plane would be out of the question. The doctor then tried to get a helicopter, but the snow had grounded them, too. The only alternative was an ambulance. The doctor insisted that a team go in the ambulance to administer emergency care if they could not control the bleeding. Of course this all seemed very scary to me, and for the first time in my life, I was thinking that there was a good chance I could lose my dearly loved husband.

The ambulance left, and I sat for another hour waiting for Lori. I became worried that, because of the snow, we might not even be able to make it to Spokane. When Lori finally arrived, I was shaking. I was so glad to see her, and so glad that she would be driving. Not only do I hate driving in the snow, but the added stress would have made it nearly impossible for me to drive myself. I'm afraid this was not one of my finest moments of trusting God, but I don't think I had ever prayed so fervently in my life.

The roads were a mess. It took us almost four hours to reach the hospital, but finally we arrived. I was hoping the news would be good. And it was. The doctor told us that the bleeding had stopped on its own (no surgery would be necessary), but they would keep him overnight just to be sure. After everything the doctor had said at the Sandpoint hospital, I was shocked at how nonchalant the Spokane doctor had been about the seriousness of the injury. He even stated that Norm might be able to go home in the morning. While he did in fact have some broken ribs, and they'd be painful, the doctor saw no reason for him to stay longer.

Well, I surely saw reasons for him to stay in the hospital, and I was not at all pleased with this doctor's evaluation. After all, if Norm was released in the morning, I would have to drive him 90 miles back to Shiloh in a snowstorm that was showing no signs of letting up. Plus we lived 30 miles from any medical facility and 90 miles from a big hospital. The roads from the ranch could be so dangerous during snowstorms, too. What if the liver started bleeding again?

Now, anyone who knows Norm well will not be surprised at the fact that *he* was delighted to be able to go home. I think he realized that his wonderful guardian angel had been hard at work. It turned out my fears were ungrounded. Norm healed beautifully and *obviously* did not buy that Morgan. A few weeks later, we did find a wonderful Morgan named "Magic." I don't believe in magic, but he was definitely the one God sent us.

Fall from the Entryway

Everyone coming to Shiloh notices a sign in the entryway that reads, "I Believe in Angels," as well as a large angel hanging on the wall. It was put there in remembrance of an extremely miraculous event. As you enter the main lodge, there is a very interesting architectural tri-level design. As you go through the front door, you enter into the entry room. That's where you can take off your muddy boots, hang your coat, etc. Then you go up a few stairs into the foyer where you either go down the stairs to the basement rooms or up to the main floor. If you are standing at the bottom of the stairs in the basement looking up to the top, you'll see that it's a long way up. Now, standing there, imagine Norm up at the very top on scaffolding, working on trim at the ceiling. That's exactly where he was when all of a sudden, the scaffolding broke.

Norm tumbled down head first—three floors. You can imagine the consequences of that fall. Well maybe not. Remember, at Shiloh we're certain we had a guardian angel getting "Hazardous Duty" pay—most likely overtime too! As Norm was falling, Don (one of our staff members) was just starting up the stairs from the basement. In that split second, Norm's shoulder landed on the soft spot of Don's shoulder, and he was able to negotiate his body so that he actually landed on his feet!

Both men were shocked, looked at each other, and with sheer amazement said, "Oh excuse me." Not even a bruise or broken bone for either man. What a miracle! I still cannot go up those stairs without thanking God for protecting Norm once again. I wonder if that guardian angel ever asked God for a new assignment.

Falling Off the Roof

Winter is not a good time to be building in Idaho, especially when it involves being on a roof, and especially on a very high steel roof covered with ice. But someone forgot to tell Norm that. So, that's exactly where he was—out on the roof of the lodge in 30-degree weather. At least he did have a rope tied around the chimney that he could grab if needed. The other thing in his favor was that he and I weren't alone on the ranch at that time. Jeff, a young man who stayed with us for several weeks to get off drugs, and a young woman with other particular needs were with us at that time. Jeff had just come in the cabin and was sitting at the wood stove in his stocking feet, trying to thaw them out, when the woman said, "Hey, come and look at this... Is Norm in trouble up there?"

When the three of us looked out the window, we could see that indeed, Norm was in big trouble. He was sliding down the roof and trying to grab the chimney rope, but it was just out of his reach. Jeff dashed out of the cabin, now in his bare feet, ran through the snow, scrambled up the ladder, got to the chimney, and flung the end of the rope to Norm. It was another guardian-angel moment... The rope went directly to Norm's hand just has he reached the edge of that roof. As he held on for dear life, Jeff pulled with all his might and was able to get Norm to a safe area. You can believe, it was a night of thankful prayers and celebration at Shiloh Ranch.

The Rolling Logs

Building Shiloh was quite an adventure, not only for Norm and me, but also for some of the workers that helped us and guests. Our first summer at Shiloh, Norm purchased a portable sawmill. The goal, since funds were very slim, was to be able to cut down some of our own trees and convert them to lumber we could use to build the barn. One morning as Norm was cutting some of the wood, the other men were prepping the logs from the cut trees so they could haul them down to Norm. Always one to protect his hearing when he was operating the noisy saw, Norm wore his earmuffs. As they were attempting to move one of the logs, it got away from them and started rolling towards Norm, who worked downhill from the men and had his back towards them.

Both men started yelling at the top of their lungs, trying to warn Norm, but with the noise of the saw and his ears covered, Norm could not hear their screams. They knew Norm's life was in extreme danger. If that log hit him, surely he would be seriously hurt if not killed. They were quite a ways up the hill from him, so the situation looked dire. But, like Superman, that guardian angel came to the rescue.

As the log quickly approached Norm, it struck a large rock that was just a few feet from him. It hit that rock at just the right angle that it caused the log to swerve to the right and miss Norm by just a foot or so. Everyone swallowed hard and breathed a great sigh of relief. As the men relayed the story to all of us, it was another evening of celebration and thankfulness for God's great protection. I know there are many times when we don't even know that God has protected us from something, but at Shiloh there were many times we personally witnessed it. Our guardian angel really did work overtime. In fact, I'm sure we had more than one looking out for us, and especially Norm.

The Big One

It was the end of August, 1997. The Shiloh Ranch summer guests were gone, our summer help had just left, and Norm and I were alone, preparing for new guests that evening. A very special couple was going to be married soon, and they had asked us to host their rehearsal dinner that night. The Cornish game hens were defrosting, and I was busy cleaning and preparing the lodge for the evening festivities. Norm was in the shop putting away the summer rafts and lifejackets. We were both tired but happy about how the summer had been. So many people came that year, and we saw so much growth in marriages and relationships with God. It really had been a rewarding summer.

After I vacuumed, I remembered that there were some things I needed from the cabin. I walked out the front door and noticed Norm standing at the door of the shop. He called to me, "Barb, come here. I need you." I figured he just wanted me to help him carry something, so I answered, "OK, I'll be there in a minute. I just need to run to the cabin first." In a tone I had *never* heard before, he hollered, "No Barb, NOW. I need you NOW!" Catching the urgency in his voice and looking closer, it became very clear that there was something terribly wrong. Blood was running down his face.

Hurrying to him, I discovered Norm was leaning hard on a creeper—the kind you use to get underneath a car. What I didn't know at first was that he had fallen from the loft of the shop, hit his head on a bench, and then landed on the cement floor of the shop on his hip. He had even bounced a couple of times on that hard cement. He couldn't walk or get up, so he lay on his stomach and pulled himself out the door, scooting on his elbows. Once he was out of the shop, he saw the creeper and somehow used it to pull himself up on the good leg. Then, he called and called for over an hour. Because of the vacuum noise and the good insulation of the log lodge, I could not hear him.

Since he had been standing there for some time, he had ample time to think about what I should do to help him. When I finally reached him, he said, "OK, Barb, I think I have broken my hip, but I want you to get the Suburban and back it up to me. Then you can open the back doors, and I can fall into it. Then, you push me the rest of the way with my good leg, close the doors and drive me to the emergency room in St. Maries."

It sounded like a good plan...until I opened the back doors of the Suburban and discovered that several 80-pound sacks of concrete were in my way. That day I think I got a pretty good understanding of how people can simply lift up a car in a dire emergency. My adrenalin was really pumping! Norm says I picked up those bags and threw them out of the van as if they were sacks of cotton. I think he wanted to say, "Whoa! That's my woman," but we weren't out of the woods yet.

I was able to get him to fall into the van but unable to push him in all the way. His legs were still hanging out the back of the van. He kept saying, "Just push me in." I was so afraid that I'd injure him even more, I just couldn't. I finally called a neighbor who came and was able to pull him in by his arms.

We drove the 30 miles to the hospital where he was x-rayed and examined. Norm has a really high pain tolerance, and because he was not demonstrating a lot of pain, the doctor didn't seem too concerned. He stitched the cut on his forehead and looked at the x-ray. The doctor said that he probably had broken his tailbone and I could take him home soon. I was appalled. How in the world would I be able to take him home when I could hardly get him there? Fortunately, the x-ray technician was concerned and suggested he take some more x-rays from different positions. After looking at the new x-rays, the doctor realized that Norm had shattered the ball of his hip and broken his pelvis in four places! That's when I learned that it was a very good thing I hadn't shoved him harder into the van. I could have actually pushed one of the broken bones into his bladder. Thank you God for stopping me from making a terrible mistake!

Well, it was now an entirely new ball game. Of all of Norm's accidents and near-accidents over the years, *this* was certainly the big one. Norm was taken by ambulance to Sacred Heart Hospital in Spokane. Then came more x-rays, more examinations and more calls to find a doctor who could perform the necessary surgery. After a couple of days, it was determined that he would actually have to be flown to Harborview Trauma Center in Seattle, and I'd be able to fly with him.

Now flying is one of my favorite hobbies. In fact, when I was young I wanted to take flying lessons. Since I was raising small children, we decided that I should put that on hold till they were grown. By the time they were gone from the home, though, we had started Shiloh, and then it just wasn't feasible. To make up for it though, Norm would arrange for me to fly in some very unique planes on my birthdays. For instance, one year I got to fly in a glider at Silverwood. The next year I got to fly in a bi-plane with goggles and all! I tried talking the pilot into letting me walk the wing. Of course he said no; the insurance apparently didn't cover that. So, you can imagine what a surprise (and delight, despite the circumstances) it was when the ambulance pulled up to a Lear Jet at the Spokane Airport.

They loaded the stretcher into the plane and then showed me where I could sit. I leaned over to Norm and said, "Oh Norm, you didn't have to go this extreme to get me a Lear Jet ride." He laughed. I sat back, and in spite of the anxiety and worry over Norm's injury, I enjoyed the ride.

Another ambulance was waiting for us in Seattle, where we were transported to Harborview. They took him past all the people in the waiting room and told me just to take a seat; they would call me when they had him in a room. There were a lot of people in that ER, though, and I immediately knew that was not where I wanted to be. It wasn't just because I wanted to be with my husband—there were some really scary thing going on. It seems that there had been a gang fight somewhere in Seattle. Some of the gang members were brought to Harborview to be treated, but some of them were also in that waiting room—and it was obvious that they were not *all* in the same gang! I just knew I was about to be in the middle of another gang fight.

After all I'd been through, that was just too much. I must have looked completely traumatized, because as soon as the attendant took one look at my face, she came over, put her arm on my shoulder, and said, "Here, now. Come with me. I don't see any reason why you shouldn't be with your husband." I totally agreed and was so happy to get out of there. Well, at least until I walked into the room and saw Norm. Then I thought maybe the waiting room was actually better.

The doctor was drilling a pin through Norm's knee. It was the kind of drill that Norm uses for drilling holes in a piece of wood. *What in the world would cause a doctor to perform such a horrible thing to a person?* I wondered if Norm was dead or something. He was just lying there, not screaming out in pain or anything. The nurse saw that my eyes were as big as when I was in the waiting room, I'm sure, only now I was white as a sheet. She scooted me out of that room into a hallway, where I sat until they took Norm to a regular hospital room.

Norm had more x-rays, more exams and was moved to all different rooms for each procedure. His tolerance for pain was beginning to wane. I didn't know it until then, but an acetabular fracture is complicated. There are not very many doctors in the United Stated that can do it, but we had the best. We had to wait three days until he could operate, though.

The operation took eight hours, but Norm came through it beautifully. Norm is a tough guy, and it paid off. He was very diligent in his therapy, too. The man in the bed next to him had the same injury, but he ended up going to a nursing home after being discharged. At that point, we were not sure if Norm would be completely healed or would even be able to work at the ranch again, but we knew God was in control. We also knew that there were many people praying for him.

One day a friend that lives in Seattle came to the hospital and wanted to know what she could do. I told her that they had cut Norm's clothing off of him when he arrived at the hospital in St. Maries, and now I needed to get to a shopping center to buy him new clothes for the trip home.

She drove me to the nearest shopping center, and as I was getting out of the car, I heard a very familiar sound. I looked up and there were a bunch of Canada geese flying right over me—honking! I knew then that Norm was going to be fine. I love how God has used those geese to encourage me.

When Norm was discharged, a wonderful friend of ours, Dr. Luther, drove another wonderful friend's van from St. Maries to Seattle and then drove us both back home to Shiloh. It was such a relief to have him there to help me get Norm up all of the stairs of the lodge into our bedroom. Norm continued to work hard at his therapy, and in November when he went back to the doctor for his final checkup, the doctor said, "Wow! You are truly a miracle." Well, we know it certainly is a miracle. We thank God for it often. Norm has never had any problem with his hip and still does crazy things that he probably shouldn't do. I'm so glad he has such a hard-working guardian angel.

Each Christmas it is a tradition in our family to watch the movie, *It's a Wonderful Life.* At the very end of the movie, after the guardian angel shows the hero how the world would have been if he had never been born, George Bailey returns home to his family—a new man with a new appreciation for his life. As he is celebrating, he hears a bell ringing on his Christmas tree. Then he remembers what the angel told him: When an angel has fulfilled the duty he had been sent to earth to do, he receives his wings and a bell rings. George realizes that Clarence (his guardian angel) has just received his wings. Of course, the Bible doesn't include this endearing tradition, but still, I wonder... If Norm's angel hasn't gotten his wings yet, he's certainly earned them!

Chapter 6

LESSONS LEARNED

God, Cars, and Me

My love for cars started at a very early age, and unfortunately, my love for God came much later. Maybe my interest in cars developed because we were probably the only family in the neighborhood who didn't own one. Finally at the age of 13, my family purchased our first car. It was an old 1939 Ford.

I will never forget the fun I had sitting behind the wheel in the driveway, pretending I was driving. It had an old stick shift on the floor. I'd put in the clutch, lightly put my foot to the gas pedal (of course, not really pushing down on it), and then let out the clutch ever so slowly. I would continue on through the gears till I was in the 3rd gear (only 3 forward gears in the old days). "Oops!" I would pretend, "There's someone crossing the street in front of me!" Then, I'd quickly step on the brake and down-shift back to first. I could do this for hours at a time...never leaving the driveway. All that practice paid off when, at the age of sixteen, I could finally take drivers education and enter the real world of driving. I passed the class with flying colors and, according to the instructor, was one of the fastest learners in the class.

I worked after school and saved my money till I was finally able to buy an "old junker" of my own. I took auto shop in school and could proudly explain to my dates how a four-cycle engine worked (intake, compression, power, exhaust...). I could tell the year and model of every car on the road. I even made the mistake of telling my mother, who knew nothing about cars, that I would always (Forever and forever!) be able to recognize the year and model of any car. Chalk that statement up to being the typical teenager who thinks they know everything. I sure have to eat my words now! When I look at the cars on the road today, many of them look just the same to me.

When Norm and I got married and moved to San Diego, we owned only one automobile. I kept hoping and hoping that we would be able to afford a 2nd car. It seemed everyone in the neighborhood owned a 2nd car, so of course, that became an obsession with me. It was during that time that

Norm rededicated his life to the Lord, though. I suddenly found myself married to a Jesus-freak who, to make matters even worse, was insistent about tithing—money that I could have used to purchase that 2nd car! Not only was I *not* interested in knowing God, now I was even *angry* that He was keeping me from my number one desire – another car. But God had a few things He wanted to teach me about cars…and about Him.

It was a few months later, after I became a Christian myself, that I developed not only a love for God, but also a love for tithing. It became one of my greatest desires. God was now number one in my life. Funny thing is God really changed my heart; soon I didn't even consider that 2nd car anymore. And that's when things started to get funny. I've come to learn that God has a delightful and amazing sense of humor.

One day Norm's parents arrived in their beautiful 1969 Oldsmobile hard top. It was in perfect shape, mostly because of the wonderful care it received from his mom and dad. Dad took care of all the mechanical things while mom kept that car spotless; she even polished the foot pedals!

A few hours after their arrival, they stated that they had just purchased a brand new car and wanted us to have the Oldsmobile. WOW! I could hardly believe my ears! All I could think of was, "Thank you, thank you God." I knew it was a gift from Him. But He wasn't done yet.

A few months later, my mom passed away. A short time before she became ill, my step-father had purchased a new Pinto. Soon after the funeral, he drove from Oakland to San Diego to visit us. One of the first things he said, after sitting down at our kitchen table, was, "I just don't want to drive anymore. I want *you* to have the Pinto, and I am going to fly home." For heaven's sake! Now we had three cars! "Thank you God!" But he still wasn't finished.

By this time, both Norm and I had become very involved in our church and were working with the youth. Sure we had three cars, but what we really needed was a van to transport the kids to and from some of the activities we did with them. One day it just so happened that a man called to tell us that he was selling his van. He wanted to know if we were interested in buying it for a very low price. We jumped at the offer, having a small savings that would actually cover the cost. God just kept providing!

That night, I knelt down and had a long talk with God. The first thing I said was, "God, I thank you for all the cars, but you can turn off the car machine. I get it now, and I am so sorry for all those times I complained about Norm giving back to you what was yours to begin with. All we have is because of you. I pray I will always put You first—before cars and before anything! I want you to be number one in my life." And you know, He just continued to speak to my heart through cars...

Years later after we had moved to the ranch and started our ministry, we purchased an old Dodge sedan. It was a good running car, but when winter came, I discovered that this car would never work in the wilds of Idaho. Our driveway was fairly steep, very narrow, and had big drop offs that would scare any novice winter-driver. One day while driving up the driveway, and after a long day of grocery shopping, I hit a patch of ice that caused the car to slide sideways toward one of those drop offs. It stopped with the driver-side tires on the very edge of the cliff. I couldn't even open my door to escape! I had to climb over to the passenger's side to get out of the car. I ran up to the cabin yelling for Norm to help me and headed immediately to the bathroom. I won't go into details there, but suffice it to say I was really scared. Norm knew immediately that I'd had a shock and a fearsome fright. After inspecting the situation, and with his very calm and level temperament, he was able to get his truck and eventually tow the car out of its precarious position.

    I decided then and there that we needed a 4-wheel-drive car. Now mind you, we didn't have much money at that time to buy one. It was another case of needing God to intervene. For several months I frequented the local car dealers, but always the price was too high or the car was too old. I really wanted a Subaru, as I had heard such wonderful things about how good they were in snow. One day, as we were having devotions in the morning after breakfast, I was bemoaning about not being able to find the car I wanted. As our ranch hand, Bill, was leaving the cabin to take out the horses, he said, "Well, have you prayed about it?" I said "Oh my gosh! Isn't that crazy? I have forgotten to pray about it, but I will now." So I did. I told God how much money we had saved towards buying a car, how we could pay $40 a month for about 6 months and could trade in our Dodge. I also expressed to Him that I really wanted a Subaru station wagon so I could carry all the supplies in it for the ranch. When Bill came in for lunch he asked if I had prayed about the car. I said yes, and that I had asked God for a 4-wheel-drive Subaru.

Bill then said, "What color did you ask for?"

"Oh Bill, I didn't tell God I wanted a certain color; that just doesn't seem right," I replied.

Bill's response was, "Well, I think sometimes you can be specific with God, and it wouldn't hurt to ask for the color you'd like."

I laughed and guessed I preferred beige as it wouldn't be as likely to show the dirt from our road as much. We began eating our lunch, and the phone rang: "Hello, Shiloh Ranch, Barbara speaking."

"This is Mr. Hanson from the Subaru dealership in Coeur d'Alene; I believe I have just the car for you." This man had been looking for the "right car" for several months to no avail.

"It's a 1981 Subaru station wagon, 4-wheel-drive, and the price is exactly what you told me you could pay."

My heart jumped for joy, but then I smiled as I thought about the color. "Mr. Hanson, I just have one question for you: What color is the car?"

"It's beige." Now I knew this was the car God had provided for us!

I said, "We'll be there in two hours."

I called Norm in and told him that this was it. God had truly provided just the car we needed. His response, having worked with many car dealers was, "Now Barb, don't get your hopes up, you know how this goes. We will probably get there, and they will look at your car and say they can't give you as much trade-in as they stated. They just didn't realize our car was in such bad condition. Or they might say they made a mistake on the price of the car."

"No, Norm; that is not going to happen. This is my car from the Lord."

Well, we proceeded to Coeur d'Alene with Norm continuing to warn me not to get my hopes up. I didn't pay any attention to him. We arrived at the dealership, and within an hour, we had signed the papers, written out our check, and purchased the best car we have ever owned. We drove that car for many years, putting thousands of miles (rough miles, I might add) on it and never had a major repair bill.

Although my desire for cars moved into more of a need for dependability and practicality over the years, I still love a good car. Mostly I love how God has used cars in my life to show me how personal He is, how He truly listens to our prayers, and how He really does provide.

Secret to Quitting Smoking

For quite some time after I became a Christian, I tried very hard to quit smoking. I knew it was bad for my health. My mom had died from lung cancer. Even the fear of that didn't keep me from enjoying those little coffin nails, as so many people called them. Actually, I became very good at quitting…week after week for several days at a time. After a while, I got pretty frustrated. I had heard so many other Christians talk about how God just took away all the desire for the cigarettes, but He hadn't taken my desire away. I always wanted them and needed them. They were my friends! I had such a hard time giving them up…for good.

With my sanguine personality, I love to talk and be around people. I recall one day when it became so obvious to me that my two "passions" were in direct conflict. We were all sitting around the table having a wonderful conversation about politics—my favorite—and I really needed a cigarette. I never smoked in the house, so I had to leave the table and go outside to enjoy the much desired cigarette. As I stood out there in the cold, puffing away, I began to resent the fact that I'd had to leave my friends and that great conversation. For the first time, I began to see that cigarette as my enemy, rather than my friend. No longer was it something I needed to *give up*, but rather, it was something that had control over me. I had always believed that I chose to smoke cigarettes because I wanted them, but suddenly I realized that I smoked them because they had a *hold* on me. I didn't want to go outside and have that cigarette right then, but I *had* to because my body said it was time.

That was the last cigarette I ever smoked. It's been years and years now, and what I learned from that experience is that we need to look at our attitude, our belief system, and our values instead of trying to change our behavior. Our values and attitudes will determine our feelings, and our feelings will determine our behavior. The real key is in letting God, through the Holy Spirit, change our attitude, belief system, and values, giving us true victory over our addictions and unhealthy behavior. If you get the engine pulling the train, the caboose will follow!

Sitting in God's Lap

I remember a bleak season in my life when my attitude was definitely not that of a wonderful, sweet-loving Christian. I didn't even want to talk to God! I knew my sin, and I was ashamed to be in His presence. One day, as I was sharing this feeling with my husband, he told me a delightful story from his childhood in Mississippi.

Every day, just before his dad would come home from work, his mother would take a bath, put on a clean starched dress, and go out onto the screened in porch to sit in the swing and snap her beans or prepare her peas for the evening meal. Mississippi is very hot and muggy during the summer, and Norm was a typical 8-year-old boy, playing in the field, catching snakes, looking for bugs, or riding his bike on the dusty trail next to his home. The dirt mixed with his sweat would form little dirty beads all over his body. Seeing his mom on the swing, he would often run to the porch and ask if he could sit on her lap. I know what my first reaction would be—"No way!" After all, his mom was all fresh and clean. But this wonderful loving mom would always put her bowl of beans or peas aside and pull him up into her lap. There they would sit, swinging and hugging. Norm would show her his "skint" knee or cut on his finger, and she would listen to how he got it, kiss it, and make it well. After a little nurturing, he would squirm down and be off again.

Norm told me this story to remind me that God is like that. No matter how dirty we are, we can always come to Him. He is perfectly clean but will pull us unto his lap and listen to our every care. What a beautiful "picture" for me to carry in my mind. Now I know that I don't have to clean up my life or my attitude before I talk to God. In fact, that's when I need him most!

Bedtime Stories from Shiloh — Barbara Lovett

The Journey vs. the Destination

I love to take trips. When I was growing up, we very seldom went on any, though. I remember a trip on a train to Salt Lake City to visit relatives and another to see my father before he went overseas during WWII. We didn't own a car, so even little trips were not a frequent occurrence. Even after I was married, we seldom took vacations. We did travel with the Navy, however. Those trips were all-nighters, as we called them; I drove all day, while Norm drove all night. Our girls finally had their first motel experience when they were in their teens. We traveled from Chicago to Albuquerque to celebrate Norm's parents' 50th anniversary. The girls almost fainted when Norm said we were going to stop at the Motel 6 for the night. As I recall, we checked in before 7 pm, so they had their first experience swimming in a motel pool, also! Truthfully, it always seemed like the destination was the most important part of a trip; the journey was just a necessity.

Several years ago, while watching an interview with the CEO of a large company, my view of "the journey" began to shift, though. The fact that the newly named CEO of this prominent company was a woman was quite newsworthy at the time. When asked about this great accomplishment, she said, "Success is in the journey, not in the destination." I was so moved by that statement that I really started to think about the journeys of my own life. Where was my focus?

When we first started Shiloh Ranch, I thought that in about five years we would have the lodge built and everything would be in place to begin the ministry. Eighteen years later I found myself lamenting to a friend, "Gosh I wish we would finish the building so we could get on with the ministry." He gave me an "Oh brother" look and said, "What do you mean? *Building* the lodge has *been* the ministry." I thought about that for a while and realized that if someone had just come in the first year, handed us a million dollars and said, "Go for it! Hire the crew, and get this done this year," we would have missed the blessings, the lessons, the growth, and the privilege of watching God work out all the details. Perhaps the worst part for me, a Sanguine, would have been that I'd have no stories to tell.

I think my friend was trying to tell me that the journey was part of the success of Shiloh's ministry. Of course, looking back, I have to agree. Destinations and goals are important. We wouldn't have journeys without them, and certainly we have reason to celebrate when a goal is reached.

I remember when we reached our twentieth year at the ranch and had finally been able to pay off the land debt. The journey to that milestone is packed full of testimonies to God's faithfulness and provision! The year after that, we finally completed the lodge. That lodge represented more than what human hands could accomplish; it was and is a *monument* to God's faithfulness. It testifies to all the priceless experiences we'd had throughout the fifteen years of building it: the lessons learned, the ways God provided and protected, the near accidents, and even the accidents and frustrations that God used to strengthen and heal us in ways we could not see. It was a long journey, but it was invaluable...and full of wonderful memories.

Sometimes the journey is needed to help us do things a step at a time. When I turned sixty, I decided to try something very new. I went scuba-diving in the ocean! I went 80 feet under for 40 minutes—a real accomplishment for me, as I had always said this was something I would never do. But my very wise husband found a way to change my tune. Norm first took me snorkeling. Once I was comfortable with that, I took the next step. He had me try "snuba-diving", which is going 10 or 20 feet under without a tank but just with a regulator hooked by a tube to the tanks above water. Then, when I was comfortable with that, I took the next step. He had me take a 2-hour scuba lesson in a pool. After obtaining my certificate for a 40-ft dive, we went out in a boat to a beautiful dive spot, and down we went.

I have to admit I was fearful, but I did it! Norm encouraged me to take it one step further, so I took the lessons to become a certified diver. I can't believe it, but I actually did it. I've been fortunate enough to scuba-dive in the Caribbean and Hawaii! If he had started with that, I would never have agreed. The journey to the bottom of the ocean has been a step-by-step process.

I believe that God doesn't want us to miss a step. The process on how we get where we are going is the important factor. A great illustration of this is written in the book *Pilgrim's Progress*. The whole story is about the journey the two main characters must make to reach the Celestial Kingdom. They have to stay on the specified path and take all the necessary steps. Along the way are many distractions and various characters, like Greed, who try to thwart them. Towards the end, they have to cross a river, but a character named Self-deception urges them to follow him. He tells them that they don't really have to *walk through* the river, that it's much easier to take a boat. Of course taking the boat would also take them off the path. Fortunately they decline and proceed through the river.

When they reach the gate of the Celestial Kingdom, they find that Self-deception is already there. Truly, traveling by boat was faster. However, when asked for the special engraved invitation, Self-deception does not have it, and they do. Arriving at their destination quickly was not actually the point; the success was in the journey.

The Big Fight

It was 8:00 in the evening. The last guest had just left. Whew! We were exhausted. It had been simply non-stop for several weeks...or had it been months? The one thing I knew was that we had not had a real day off all summer. My goal for the night was to get myself into a hot bubble bath, cut my toenails, and spend some quality time with my husband. I can't even remember the last time we'd had the time to just sit and talk about something that didn't have to do with Shiloh. And the toenails! Oh my gosh; that was really a sore point for me. Just thinking about it reminded me of the day when I was putting on my sandals and noticed my "claws." I looked down and was appalled at how long my toenails had gotten. Why, the horses had better trimmed feet than me. It just seemed that every night when I would go back to our quarters, I would look at them and think, "Oh maybe tomorrow night. I am just too tired tonight. I want to go to bed." The problem was "tomorrow night" didn't come.

One day someone who was staying at the ranch for a while mentioned some things that I might want to consider doing—to improve ministry. Well, that definitely pushed my button. Sadly, my response was not what it should have been. Clearly offended, I said, "Excuse me, but I cannot and absolutely will not do that until I can have some 'cut-toe-nail time!'" Fortunately she was a good friend and was not offended. Needless to say, they were long, and I do mean long, overdue. It really had been a full summer.

As I was running the hot water for my much awaited bath that evening, the phone rang. "Shiloh Ranch, Barbara speaking..."

"Oh, Barbara, I am so glad I caught you. This is Jane. Dick and I have just had a terrible fight, and I think he is considering a divorce. After a long talk, he did say that if we could come up and talk to you guys tonight, he would reconsider. Could we please come right now?"

I politely told her I had to check with Norm, but at the same time I was thinking to myself,

"Well there goes my bath. I *really* don't want to listen to another person's marriage problems." I did check with Norm, and he said yes they could come on up. Finally, after a couple of hours, we were able to get to bed—no bath, no "cut-toe-nail time."

Although I eventually got after my toenails, this type of scenario continued for several more months. Slowly my attitude and disposition changed to the point that I dreaded having guests, even resented them. One night while I was on the phone with a woman, whose marriage was in big trouble, I was seething on the inside. All I could think was, "I can't listen to one more complaint about her husband or one more problem. I am sick of other people's problems. When do I get to talk about mine?"

Then, an idea came to my mind. I wanted to hang up on her, but I knew I couldn't do that unless it seemed like we had just been disconnected. So, in the middle of one of my sentences, I pushed the button to disconnect. Because I did it while I was talking, I was convinced she would believe it was caused by something gone wrong with the connection. Then, I just left the phone off the hook the rest of the evening. After all, we lived in the wilderness, bad phone connections could happen at any time. Right? Right!

Well, that was the beginning of our season of burnout. Norm had reached it, too. Unfortunately, neither of us recognized it, and because of the busy schedules we kept, we really never took the time to share our feelings with each other. Finally, one Sunday during the winter months, it all came to a head, though.

It had just snowed the day before, and then everything turned to ice. The road from the ranch to Calder was horrible! It had steep cliffs with no guard rails. In some places it was so narrow that two cars couldn't pass, and scattered on the road, often there were big rocks that had fallen from the hillside above. Any wrong move and you could easily slide off and be severely injured—even plunge to your death. That was what was on my mind that early Sunday morning as we were driving to church. Isn't the drive to church where most arguments happen, anyway?

When I say, "we" were driving, I mean Norm was driving. And Norm did not share the same fear that I had of that mountain road. Consequently, he wasn't driving it as cautiously as I wanted. So, of course, I became an obnoxious back-seat driver. Just perhaps a half mile from Calder, one of the tires hit a rock in the road, and I yelled at him to slow down. This time I had pushed his last button, and he yelled back at me, "Barbara, just shut up!" Whoa. Well, my first thought was, "How dare he yell at me like that!"

"Norman, just stop and let me out of the car," I spewed. To my surprise, instead of saying he was sorry for yelling at me, he stopped the car and said, "Fine, get out." Just like that! Well, what to do now...? I had really put myself in a corner, but I wasn't about to back down. So, I foolishly got out of the car, and he drove off. As soon as I put boots to the ground, I realized I was going to have to walk three miles back...and I wasn't in boots. I looked down at my impractical heels, already slipping sideways on that icy road, and then back up at the tail end of our car as it disappeared around a corner. Then I relaxed and thought, "No, Norm surely will come back for me in just a minute. He just wants to make a point." But five minutes and then ten minutes passed...and still no Norm. I had managed to walk about the equivalency of two blocks, but it was not without slipping and falling on the ice several times. I was mad and hurt and more than a little bit stunned.

Finally, after about fifteen minutes, I heard something behind me and turned around. It wasn't our car, but it *was* Norm. He was walking and obviously trying to catch up with me. He proceeded to explain to me how God had been talking with him. After I jumped out of the car, he had driven down the rest of the way to Calder, all the time praying that another car would turn up the road where he'd just left me, because he was sure they would pick me up and drive me back home. But no luck; there was no one else out that morning. He started across the bridge, and all of a sudden the car died. He kept trying to get it started, but again, no luck. Now remember, we don't really believe in luck.

As he pushed the car to the side of the road, he began praying to God for guidance. He felt sure God was telling him to "walk back up that road and find your wife." Then he knew God wanted us to spend the time walking home together talking it out. As I recall, that morning he had decided to wear some old Cowboy boots that didn't really fit him well. He'd figured since he would just be driving to church and back, he'd use the opportunity to stretch them out a bit. Well, you can imagine how uncomfortable he was climbing a few miles up that icy hill in wet boots that were way too tight. I'm sure we were both quite a sight!

God knew just what the two of us needed that wintery morning. That walk home was the best thing we had done in months. Finally, we had time for us to just reconnect and talk about all the things that had been bothering us. That's when we became quite aware that there was a good possibility we were in, or fast approaching, burnout and needed help.

When we got home, we called our Pastor from Illinois, and he told us he would fly out that week for a few days. His visit was an absolute breath of fresh air, and there was one particular principle he taught us that really helped keep us going another 25 years. I believe it's a very important principle for anyone, but especially those in the ministry, who finds himself in burnout mode. He explained it like this:

So many of us believe that we have to live our lives like the song, "Jesus, Others and You." We think we're always at the bottom of the totem pole, the lowest priority. Really, as Christians, Jesus should always be sustaining and permeating our lives, but we need to make sure, as individuals, that we are healthy emotionally, spiritually, and physically. In other words, I need to make sure I have time for me, time for my hobby or interest, time to read a good book or whatever it is that brings me joy. I need to be spiritually healthy, setting aside time for my private devotions, time to be involved with church activities and just time alone with God. I also need to look after my physical health, like getting enough rest, taking care of my body (including cut-toe-nail time), going to the doctor when I'm sick, etc. If I am taking care of myself in those ways, then I can give to my husband from a place of strength and well-being.

Next, we also have to make sure our marriage is healthy emotionally, spiritually and physically. Norm and I need to have *our* time together just talking, going on a date, hiking our mountain, playing a game together, or just sitting on the deck holding hands. Then, we need to be spiritually healthy as a couple. We need our devotion times together in the morning, our praying together, going to church together, and seeking God's will together. Finally, we need to be physically healthy together. We need to be able to keep our sex life active and enjoyable, as well as make the effort to hold hands, hug and show our love for one another throughout the day. Then, we will operate as a healthy team, with the strength needed to minister to others. Our problem had been that we could never say *no* to anyone, even if it meant causing havoc in our own lives. We knew that would have to change.

After our pastor left to go back to Illinois, we sat down with the calendar and marked some days for us to have a "date." If someone called and said they needed to come and see us that day, we would just tell them, "Oh, I'm sorry, we have something already scheduled for that day. Could you come the next day?" I was surprised at first, because the next day or any other day seemed to work just fine. It was actually quite simple, and boy did it make a difference.

Sometimes I wonder whether we'd be celebrating our 45th wedding anniversary this year if we hadn't received that advice. I thank God that we finally ran into burnout, because without it, we may not have learned this valuable lesson. We might never have known how rich our lives and our marriage could really be.

Oh, and by the way, when Norm went back to Calder to work on the car, so that it could be driven home, it started up right away. No work necessary. God sure does have a sense of humor. And I'm glad Norm and I can still laugh about it together today.

God, Prayers, and Sanguines

Being sanguine, I have always viewed God as a very loving and affectionate Father. I sometimes tend to be more informal than I probably should. For the most part, I am cheerful and hopeful, looking for the fun in life.

I remember one time as I was preparing to take a coffee break, I asked God if He would like to join me. I then proceeded to sit down and converse with Him as if He were there in the room with me (which, by the way, I am sure He was - just not drinking coffee). I remember rambling on and on and then realizing that I was not giving Him the opportunity to talk—typical sanguine behavior. Finally, I stopped and placed the imaginary tape over my mouth. I purposefully just sat and listened to what He had to say to me. It was a sweet time, the highlight of my day. He had much to say to me, and all of it was invaluable to my situation at that time. I guess my problem has always been that I talk too much. That was, after all, the first comment on my report card in the 1st grade: "Barbara is a good student, but Barbara talks too much." God is so patient with me.

I remember being in a group of believers who decided one day that instead of our normal prayer time, we would all sit for 30 minutes in complete silence and just listen to God. You can bet the person who came up with that idea was not a Sanguine! As I sat there, I kept catching myself telling God all that was on my mind. Then I'd remember, "No, we are supposed to be listening to God," and I'd pull back on my mouth reigns and try again. After about five minutes of quieting my mind, God said, "Barbara, I love you." Wow, that was worth being quiet for, and it motivated me to be quiet again. Again, God said, "Barbara, I love you." Being quiet can be quite rewarding.

I discovered in that thirty minutes that God's love for me motivated me to be quiet and just listen to Him. Then it struck me; we can also motivate others by our love. Pure and simple, my love could motivate. It was quite a timely lesson for me. I had been struggling with how to motivate a certain person to do the right thing. My default was to lecture them about what was right and wrong in a given situation. And believe me, I probably would have gone on for hours and would have accomplished nothing except to make them pull away from me. God's message was to just love them for now; that would be motivation enough.

Chapter 7

THE LEGACY OF SHILOH

Our Darkest Days

Throughout our years at Shiloh, I witnessed so many times when God used what I considered a bad situation and turned it around for something good. There were times when God did not answer my prayer, and later I discovered it was for my own good. I would thank him for *not* giving me what I wanted or thought I needed. Isn't it amazing how we think we are so wise, have the right answers and then demand God do it our way?

One of the darkest times we ever had at Shiloh was when we decided exactly how things would go, how the ministry should succeed, and step-by-step how God should make these things happen. We wanted our way. They weren't bad plans or evil plans. Actually, they were quite wonderful plans. But they were not God's plans.

After building the ministry at Shiloh for almost 25 years, our biggest desire was that when we were too old to continue, another couple would come and take over. That way all that we had built, the ministry to families, would continue. Of course we had a timetable for that, too. One, or perhaps even two couples, would come on staff, we imagined. For a year or so they'd work alongside us, learning the ropes. Then we would retire, and Shiloh would continue on strengthening and restoring marriages just like our brochure stated.

We prayed that God would send us the right couple, so we started the search. Many couples applied. Several didn't meet the requirements. Several didn't think they'd be able to adapt to the "wilderness" living. Some of the questions they would ask were, "Do you get cell-phone service here?" and "What about high-speed internet?" Unfortunately, I would have to explain, "No, matter of fact, it wasn't too long ago that we had a 4-party line and no call-waiting, and we just have the really slow dial-up internet." Their eyes would really get big when I had to explain that it was 6 miles to the post office, 30 miles to the nearest hospital, grocery store, or gas station, and actually 90 miles to the nearest shopping center. Oh, then when I told them the salary and the hours we worked, they actually ran. We continued to advertise the position in many different venues.

One day we received a call from a couple who had seen the ad and were very interested in the position. After a very positive conversation on the telephone, we made arrangements to visit them at their home. From the minute we entered their home, I just really felt like this was the couple we had been waiting so long for. At the end of the evening, we planned a time for them to come and see the ranch. They did come, and it just seemed to convince us even more that God had finally answered our prayers. They met with the board of directors who also gave the stamp of approval. Soon after that, they packed all their things and moved to the ranch. The next nine months were exciting and busy. Besides all the guests we had that year, Norm was preparing to start building our home in Post Falls, Idaho. We were delighted that Shiloh would continue after we left.

Then, in February, the ball fell. They say all bad things happen in 3's, and although I am not at all superstitious, I must admit that month there were three devastating events in our lives. The first was that our wonderful couple very unexpectedly left, deciding that the ministry was not what they had expected. We were heartsick. We didn't know what we were going to do because we had already begun our retirement plans. The 25th anniversary of Shiloh celebration had to be canceled. Building plans on our home had to be delayed. The disappointment was overwhelming, and we grieved the loss. We had grown to really love this couple.

A few days after the couple left, we were hit with the news that my daughter had decided to divorce her husband and move to Chicago, taking all of our grandchildren with her. We were devastated, and the irony made it even worse. Here we were trying to strengthen and restore marriages and our own daughter was getting a divorce. How could this happen? We felt like complete failures. And of course here we were on the verge of being able to finally move close to them—or so we'd thought—finally have all that time to spend with them. I'd looked so forward to going to my grandson's soccer games, taking my granddaughters shopping, having lots of family dinners together. Those dreams were gone.

Finally, the 3rd disaster came just a few days later. It had been very cold outside, but as I looked out from my cabin window one morning, I noticed that all the windows in the lodge were steamed up and there were icicles hanging off the decks. It seemed impossible as even though it was cold, we hadn't had any snow that would cause icicles. I ran up to the lodge, and as I entered I realized it was flooded. There was hot water everywhere.

The basement was flooded, the upstairs guest bedrooms were flooded, and the water had reached almost to the living room and kitchen. I walked through the water in the basement and opened the door to one of the guest bedrooms. The ceiling had fallen in from all the water from the floor above. I yelled for Norm. When he started inspecting the rooms, he realized that a hot water pipe in one of the upper bedrooms had broken. Since we had instant hot water heaters, the hot water just continued for hours and hours. What a mess.

I called one of our neighbors, and she and her son came up and spent half the day helping us move furniture out of the rooms. We knew the cleanup of all the water was impossible for us, so we called a company in Coeur d'Alene to come out. They couldn't come for another 4 or 5 hours, but when they did come and put those incredible machines to work, they sucked up all the water out of the building in just a few hours. They stayed until after midnight and then left the machines running for days to dry everything out. It took a couple of months of hard work to restore and rebuilt the rooms that had been damaged, but it could have been so much worse.

We tried to keep the ministry going for several months, but it was time for us to retire. The board hired another couple, but they also didn't work out. Finally the board of directors made the decision to put the ranch on the market. We hired a caretaker to live on the ranch to care for the horses and the property. He could only stay a year, but we were convinced the ranch would sell in that time frame. But we were now in the middle of the recession, so consequently, there were no buyers. The caretaker had to leave. Without a caretaker, the next step had to be to sell the horses and other assets. This was the hard part for us, especially when we had to sell the horses.

Norm had so much time and love invested in them. Most of them had been born on the ranch, trained by Norm, and especially loved by Norm. Whenever a foal was born, Norm would pick it up. It would struggle for a few seconds and then finally discover that Norm was stronger than they were. He would do that every day until they were too heavy for him to lift. Because of that, the foal would bond to Norm and as that foal would grow to a 1,000 pound horse it still thought Norm was stronger than it was. Norm would many times use that example to teach a principle of parenting. As parents, we need to gain the respect from our children when they are little, so that when they grow up and are even bigger than us, the respect will still be apparent. I remember taking pictures of Norm out in the pasture, sitting on the grass with a little foal across his lap and the mama just standing next to him, watching with complete trust.

After selling the horses, we had a huge estate sale to sell the other assets. People came from all over the area, and it was a very successful sale. What didn't sell was then donated to the Real Life Ministries Thrift Store in Post Falls. Our plan was after selling the ranch property and all the assets, we would roll the 501C(3) ministry over into a tax-except foundation to help other family ministries.

Month after month went by and still there were no buyers for the ranch. Then one day, as Norm and I were lamenting over the lack of a buyer, Norm said, "Barb, I wonder if Real Life Ministries would be interested in the ranch. We could just donate it to them."

"Oh, they are such a huge church, Norm. I can't imagine that they would be able to use it," I replied, reminding him that the lodge could only accommodate about 20 or 25 people at a time and

Real Life had about 8,000 people attending the church each weekend.

"That could be true, Barb, but let's at least write them a letter and offer it to them," he suggested. So we did. A couple of months went by, and we didn't hear anything back. We assumed it was just another dead-end.

I remember a time when the thought of leaving Shiloh Ranch was so overwhelming to me. We had loved the 25 years there. We had loved the ministry to families. We had loved living in the wilderness. We had loved watching people come to know the Lord. We had loved watching marriages be restored. We had loved taking people on canoe and rafting trips. We had loved teaching God's principles for marriage and parenting. I thought I would never want to leave Shiloh, BUT after those last few months, I must admit, I was SO ready to leave. I had no idea what God planned for Shiloh, but I was finally ready to let go of it all. And that is just the state of mind I believe God wanted us to be in.

The Light Shines Again

Norm and I had great plans for retirement, passing off the ministry and legacy of Shiloh, and spending the much awaited time with family, but *our plans* all seemed to have fallen apart at our feet. Oh, we had retired; it just didn't feel at all like we had imagined it. But God wasn't done with us yet...and He wasn't done with Shiloh either. The time had come for God to finally have His way with us. He had a plan all along, and believe me, it was so much better than any plan we had devised.

One day we received a call from Real Life Ministries saying that the Elders would like to meet with us to discuss our offer to donate the ranch to the church. We called our board, and Bill Westrate our chairman flew out from Chicago. We were excited. Everyone was excited. There were lots of particulars to be worked out, so much to discuss. God was in charge, though, and all the planning, details—everything just came together! We celebrated, signed all the legal papers, and finally knew that *this* was the reason for all the, what we might call, "bad things" happening in that last year. I know with all my heart that God's plan was for Real Life to have Shiloh Ranch. I also know that God had to help Norm be willing to leave the ranch, to really let go. It had been our life for over 25 years. It would have been difficult to completely turn it over to someone else. We needed an attitude change, and that last year gave us the push we desperately needed.

A few months ago, God gave us the desire of our hearts for Shiloh. We had so wanted the legacy of restoring marriages to continue through ministry at Shiloh. We had worked so hard to establish the ranch, and we didn't want it to end with us. So, as we were leaving church service one day, one of the Real Life Ministry pastors—the pastor over the marriage ministry—came up to me and put his face very close to mine. He said, "Barbara, I know that there must have been many, many people through the years praying for marriages to be saved at Shiloh Ranch, because, let me tell you, we can feel the Holy Spirit working there. We have been running a program called "911" up there, for couples about to be divorced.

They come for a weekend, and the miracles we are seeing are absolutely incredible. God is doing such a healing there. Marriages are being saved! Those prayers are being answered. God continues to want the purpose of Shiloh to be restoring and strengthening marriages. God is at work at Shiloh..."

Well, you can imagine what a glorious feeling that was to hear. It brought tears to my eyes. In fact, it still brings tears to my eyes as I am writing this. The legacy of Shiloh carries on.

*I praise God for the wonderful years He gave us to minister to His people. I want to thank Him for all His faithfulness through those years. I want to thank Him for all the faithful people who supported us and prayed for us during those 25 years at Shiloh. I want to thank Him for all the lessons we learned and for giving us what we needed, not what we wanted. Thank you Lord, for the **best years of our lives**...*

Epilogue

Norm and I have now been retired from Shiloh for six years. We live in a beautiful home on 20 acres in Post Falls, overlooking the lovely Rathdrum Prairie. It feels like we still live in the wilderness, but we are only five minutes from town.

Lori and her four adult children live in this area, and now we have two great grandchildren! We so love being able to spend time with them all. I was even able to be at the hospital when the 2nd great grandchild was born. Michele lives in California with her husband and two sons. We really treasure the times we're able to get together with them.

Never able to really sit still, I have worked for the local election board for the last couple years, and I've recently helped start a new ministry called, "Project Freedom: Adapting Homes for the Brave." We're looking for veterans with special needs, so we can adapt their homes. I'm really excited to see what God is going to do with that; our first fundraising event is coming up very soon.

Norm has a part-time job as a handyman for some area condo units. He continues to work hard at home, too, planting trees and building things. He still gets himself into high places, but now he uses professional scaffolding. Thank heavens!

Norm and I have had some wonderful opportunities to travel during our retirement years. We especially enjoy cruises. Last Spring we went on a cruise to Europe and were able to go on a 10-day tour of Israel. What a dream come true! It was so exciting to walk where Jesus walked. That was the trip of a lifetime.

Known to love parties, I continue to use our home to host many groups, families, and friends. We've had a wedding in our new home, as well as a few wedding dinners. We've been able to host several "Meet-and-Greet" events for political people running for office.
We also host our small group from church, and Norm always does a Bible study during the summer months. We call our home "Shiloh II"

because of all the previous Shiloh guests who now come to our home to see us. It's so wonderful to stay in touch.

Beau, our 4 year old Shih Tzu, fits in well with our lifestyle. All I have to say to him is, "Company is coming," and he goes to the front door, anxiously ready to greet them.

To our great delight, Shiloh continues to be a place where marriages are built up and healed. Real Life Ministries provides a variety of marriage retreats at Shiloh, and we are so pleased to be a part of the marriage mentoring team. Every month RLM hosts a retreat focusing on marriage essentials. A team of volunteer marriage mentors facilitate these. Couples come with marriages in all shapes and sizes. The vast majority of the couples attending these retreats are RLM community home group leaders, coaches, and staff. I am especially pleased that, because the ranch was donated to Real Life Ministries, there is no charge for the RLM staff. So far, over 150 couples have attended, and there's been tremendous fruit from these retreats.

RLM also provides a marriage enrichment retreat for couples who have been married 15 – 20 years or so that just need to be energized and another retreat for troubled marriages. A crisis retreat weekend, called "911," is offered for couples who are ready to sign the divorce papers. It is really a "make-it-or-break-it" last effort.

Bill Krause, the marriage pastor from RLM, tells me there have been many breakthroughs at these retreats. Marriages are being strengthened and revitalized. Many couples with difficult marriages leave motivated to take the next step in healing and reconciliation, either with counseling or through the church mentoring program.

Bill says he can feel God's presence at Shiloh and is convinced that Shiloh has truly been God-ordained as a place to save marriages. He is so thankful that it didn't end up being bought by someone who would just turn it into a hunting camp—or anything other than the purpose God had it for.

Shiloh has also been used to serve and minister to the surrounding community, providing food and clothing for anyone in need and small group Bible studies for anyone wanting to come. This past Easter, over 60 people came for services and fellowship. Many stayed until 10 p.m.!

God's plan really is better than ours. We are so blessed.